雲南鐵路博物館

文物精萃

The Essence of Cultural Relics of Yunnan Railway Museum

昆明铁路局

Kunming Railway Administration

中国铁道出版社

CHINA RAILWAY PUBLISHING HOUSE

前言

云南，简称滇，是中国西南边陲的一个内陆省份，域内高山叠叠，险流绵绵，道路难行。马匹驮运茶叶行走大山小路形成的“茶马古道”正是云南古老交通贸易方式的典型写照。

这种延续了千百年“山间铃响马帮来”的交通方式，因1910年3月31日全线建成通车的“滇越铁路”而发生了涅变。这条凝聚着欧洲法兰西技术和中国及越南劳工血汗的铁路，从北部湾的越南海防港一直北上抵达中国云南昆明。它以原始的殖民奢望与豪夺，无情地撕开了云南大山阻隔的门户，但也在随之的历史进程中客观地带来了大海之外世界的先进思想和技术信息，促成了古滇之地以蒸汽火车为前奏、以铁路运输为主旋律、从传统农耕文明向现代工业文明的华丽转身。

百余年间，以滇越铁路为开端的云南铁路，深刻影响着云南的变化与发展，也因生于斯长于斯的云南山水人文滋养而形成了自己别具一格的风情和灵性，书写出米轨、寸轨和准轨铁路“三轨并行”的独特历史，演绎了滇越铁路、个碧石铁路、成昆铁路等闻名遐尔的动人故事和传奇。

我们从云南铁路百年发展历程积淀的大量历史文献典籍和云南铁路博物馆收藏展示的万余件文物展品中，萃取部分珍品，按照机车车辆、勘测设计、线路设备、通信信号、配件工具、铭牌标志、票证票据、钱币债券、典籍章制、文化遗存、文物保护单位共11个章节，编辑成《云南铁路博物馆文物精萃》，让读者您从这部文物图册所记录的云南铁路历史印记中，聆听历久弥新的百年故事，领略神韵飞扬的铁路传奇，同我们一道筑就磅礴发展的云南铁路之梦！

Preface

Yunnan Province, briefly named "Dian", is an inland province in southwest of China where overlapping mountains and dangerous streams are continuous, making roads tough and difficult. Horses transported tea along rugged mountain paths, forming "the Ancient Tea-Horse Road", which exactly serves as a vivid portrayal of transportation and trade in ancient Yunnan.

Caravan bells had been ringing in mountains for thousands of years. This situation changed dramatically by the opening of "the Yunnan-Vietnam Railway" on March 31, 1910. Mixed up by not only technologies of Europe but also the blood and sweat of Chinese and Vietnam labors, the railway started from Vietnam Beibu Gulf(Tokyo Gulf) Hai Phong seaport and marched north to Kunming, the capital of Yunnan province. With wild colonial ambition and predatory, this railway relentlessly broke down mountain barriers of Yunnan. Objectively however, it also brought in advanced thoughts and technologies overseas. From then on, steam locomotives and railway transportation played a prelude of a crucial turn in this ancient land from traditional farming civilization to the modern industrial civilization.

Stemming from "the Yunnan-Vietnam Railway", Yunnan railway has profound impact on the changes and development of Yunnan for more than a hundred years. In return, it has also been nourished by the particular landscape and humanities bred here, thus forming its unique style and spirituality, creating the special history of three kinds of railway (1000mm gauge, 600mm gauge, and 1435mm gauge) in parallel, and performing many popular and touching legends about Yunnan-Vietnam Railway, Gejiu-Bisezhai-Shiping Railway and Chengdu-Kunming Railway etc.

We have selected some rare treasures from the mass of historical documents left by hundreds of years, and more than 10000 pieces of cultural relics shown in Yunnan Railway Museum, to compile "The Essence of Cultural Relics of Yunnan Railway Museum". These treasures are shown in eleven chapters including 1) Locomotives and Vehicles, 2) Surveys and Designs, 3) Railway Tracks, 4) Communications and Signals, 5) Parts and Tools, 6) Nameplates and Signs, 7) Tickets and Bills, 8) Currencies and Debentures, 9) Ancient Books and Records, 10) Cultural Remains and 11) Units of Cultural Relics Protection. With the historic marks of Yunnan railway displayed in this album, we hope to guide you through long-lasting stories and glamorous legends, to chase the dream of majestic development of Yunnan railway!

云南铁路博物馆

简介

云南铁路博物馆位于云南省昆明市北京路昆明北站，是以云南铁路修建和发展历史为主题的行业性专题博物馆，由昆明铁路局投资兴建，始建于1990年，2003年升格为博物馆，2014年扩建为新馆。

新扩建的博物馆，总规划用地面积14262平方米，占地面积4359平方米，建筑面积7963平方米，布展面积5155平方米，收藏或展示文物、文献万余件。博物馆由南馆和北馆组成，南馆以百年滇越铁路“云南府站”法式古典建筑为原型，北馆为萃取高铁旅客车站元素的现代建筑，两馆之间贯连一座铁路钢架桥梁，跨越车站的三条股道，将博物馆与运营中的车站组成一个整体。纵观这一建筑，仿佛一列现代列车停靠在具有悠久历史的车站，正在整装待发。从高空鸟瞰，博物馆和车站，又神似一个“工”字形的铁路钢轨剖面。整个建筑的铁路元素十分显目，博物馆的特质也非常鲜明，完美体现了古典与现代有机结合、历史与未来和谐照应的精妙构思。全新的博物馆以它独特的建筑语汇，用车站的运营活化了博物馆的历史，又以博物馆的文物烘托出车站的文化底蕴，让历史与现实亲近对话，用富有鲜活生命的运营铁路诠释历久弥新的历史文化，升华出云南铁路“从历史深处驶来、向时代远方奔去”的主题思想和意境！

云南铁路博物馆因其独特的历史和文化价值，已被命名为全国青少年教育基地、全国铁路和云南省爱国主义教育基地以及云南省科普教育基地。

Introduction to Yunnan Railway Museum

Yunnan Railway Museum is located at Kunming North Railway Station, Beijing Road, Kunming, Yunnan. It was built by Kunming Railway Administration in 1990 as an industry theme museum about the construction and development history of Yunnan railway. Then it was promoted to a museum in 2003, and newly expanded in 2004.

With a total planning area of 14262 square meters, the new museum has a covering area of 4359 square meters, a construction area of 7963 square meters and an exhibition area of 5155 square meters. More than ten thousands of pieces of cultural relics are collected and displayed in the museum. The museum is composed by South and North Hall. The South Hall is built by imitating the French classical architecture of "Yunnan Fu Station" a hundred years ago on Yunnan-Vietnam Railway, while the North Hall shows itself as a modern architecture with elements of a high-speed railway station. Between those two halls lies a steel bridge that leaps over three tracks, merging the museum and the station currently in operation into a whole one. From a wide view of this building, it seems as if a modern train berths at a historical station, ready to set out. From a bird-eye view moreover, this building together with the station is quite similar to an "I"-shaped cross-section of a rail. In the whole building, sparkle the elements of railway and qualities of museum in a perfect manner where classic and modern styles combine organically, as if history and future connect in delicate harmony. With its unique architectural verse, the new museum makes the history alive through the operation of station; in return, the modern station shows itself rich in cultural heritage because of the relics exhibited in the museum. When history closely dialogues with the reality, the enduring culture is interpreted by operating rail station with fresh vital, in which the idea and prospect become clear that coming from deep history, the Yunnan railway is running far to embrace the future!

Due to its unique historic and cultural values, Yunnan Railway Museum has been named "the National Youth Education Base", "the National Railway and Yunnan Patriotism Education Base" and "Yunnan Popular Science Education Base".

目录

Content

In 1764, a British called James Watt invented the world's first steam engine. In 1814, another British called George Stephenson improved the steam engine into the world's first steam locomotive, running on rails. On September 27, 1825, the first public commercial railway was opened between Stockton and Darlington in the United Kingdom. Stephenson made an era debut of steam locomotives by personally driving a train ordered "NO.1" of speed of 24 kilometers per hour, with a journey of 31.8 kilometers and 450 passengers. In this magnificent feat in science and technologies, humans saw a leap from farming society to industrial society. No doubt, the train became one of the most iconic stars of industrial revolution in 19th century and 20th century. Meantime, the steam locomotives broke into Yunnan with historic storms, leading Yunnan to step from agricultural civilization to industrial civilization.

Since the birth of the narrow-gauge railway in 1910, experiencing the crucial difficult in late Qing Dynasty, the hardship in old Chinese Republic, a vigorous development of new China and great leaps on the background of reform and opening, Yunnan railway nowadays is entering a new era of high-speed vehicles(EMU).

Yunnan Railway Museum faithfully records the history of past century with locomotives that cover three different gauges (1000mm, 600mm and 1435mm gauge) and equipped with four generations of engines (steam, diesel, electricity and high-speed railway) .

第1章 Article first

机车车辆

Locomotives and Vehicles

1764年，英国人詹姆斯·瓦特发明了世界第一台蒸汽机，1814年，英国人乔治·斯蒂芬森将蒸汽机组装在轨道上行走，成为世界第一台蒸汽火车。1825年9月27日，在英国斯托克顿~达灵顿间，开通了世界第一条公共商业运营铁路，斯蒂芬森亲自驾驶时速24千米、行程31.8千米、载客450名、编号No.1的列车，完成了蒸汽火车划时代的首秀。这一科学技术的壮举，使人类从农耕社会迅速飞跃进入了工业社会。无疑，火车的出现成为了19世纪和20世纪工业革命最具标志性的“明星”。而裹挟着历史风云撞进云南的蒸汽火车，也成为了牵引云南从农耕文明迈向工业文明的先驱。

自1910年诞生窄轨铁路以来，云南铁路历经清朝末年的举步维艰、中华民国的艰难困苦、新中国的蓬勃发展和改革开放的突飞猛进，而今已迈向了高速动车的崭新时代。

云南铁路博物馆陈列的机车车辆，用米轨、寸轨、准轨三种轨距的铁路和蒸汽、内燃、电力和动车的四代牵引动力，忠实地记录了这段百年发展的历史。

越滇
MICHELIN
ZZ-E1 CE

001 “米其林”内燃动车组（一级文物）

法国制造的载客胶轮内燃动车，于1914年在滇越铁路使用，1932年法国米其林公司为该车换装上橡胶轮子，成为开行在铁路上的“米其林汽车”。该车轨距1米，分主车和行李拖车两部分，车长19.7米，宽2.6米，自重8吨，牵引动力为汽油内燃发动机，功率117千瓦，行驶时速100千米。车内配软座19个，硬座24个，设有餐厨、洗卫等生活设施，是当时先进的高级公务车。

"Michelin" Diesel Multiple Units（National Grade-one Cultural relic）

The French-made rubber-tire passenger diesel locomotive was used on Yunnan-Vietnam Railway in 1914. Equipped with rubber tires by the French Company Michelin in 1932, it became a "Michelin Car" running on the rail. This car fits in with one-meter gauge, composed of main carriage and luggage carriage. It is 19.7 meters long, 2.6 meters wide and weighs 8 tons. Equipped with a traction power of petrol internal combustion engines of 117 watts, it can go 100 kilometers per hour. Fully equipped with living facilities such as 19 soft seats, 24 hard seats, kits and washrooms, it served as an advanced business train at that time.

The Steam Locomotive for 600mm Gauge（National Grade-one Cultural Relic）

The SN steam locomotive made by Baldwin Locomotive Works of the Philadelphia U.S.A in 1923 (axial model of 0-5-0) is 15000mm long, 2400mm wide and 3120mm high. This car is for 600mm gauge. The deadweight of the car is 24.95 tons with an attached coal and water carriage of 6.69 tons. The traction modulus of the car is 6691kg with a design speed of 45km per hour. The car was used on Gejiu-Bisezhai-Shiping Railway in 1926 and stopped its operation on 1st January, 1991.

002 SN型29号寸轨蒸汽机车（一级文物）

美国费城鲍尔温机车厂1923年生产的SN型（轴形排列0-5-0）蒸汽机车，长15000毫米，宽2400毫米，高3120毫米，轨距600毫米，主车自重24.95吨，附属煤水车自重6.69吨，模数牵引力6691千克，构造速度45千米/小时。1926年起运用在个碧石铁路线上，于1991年1月1日停运。

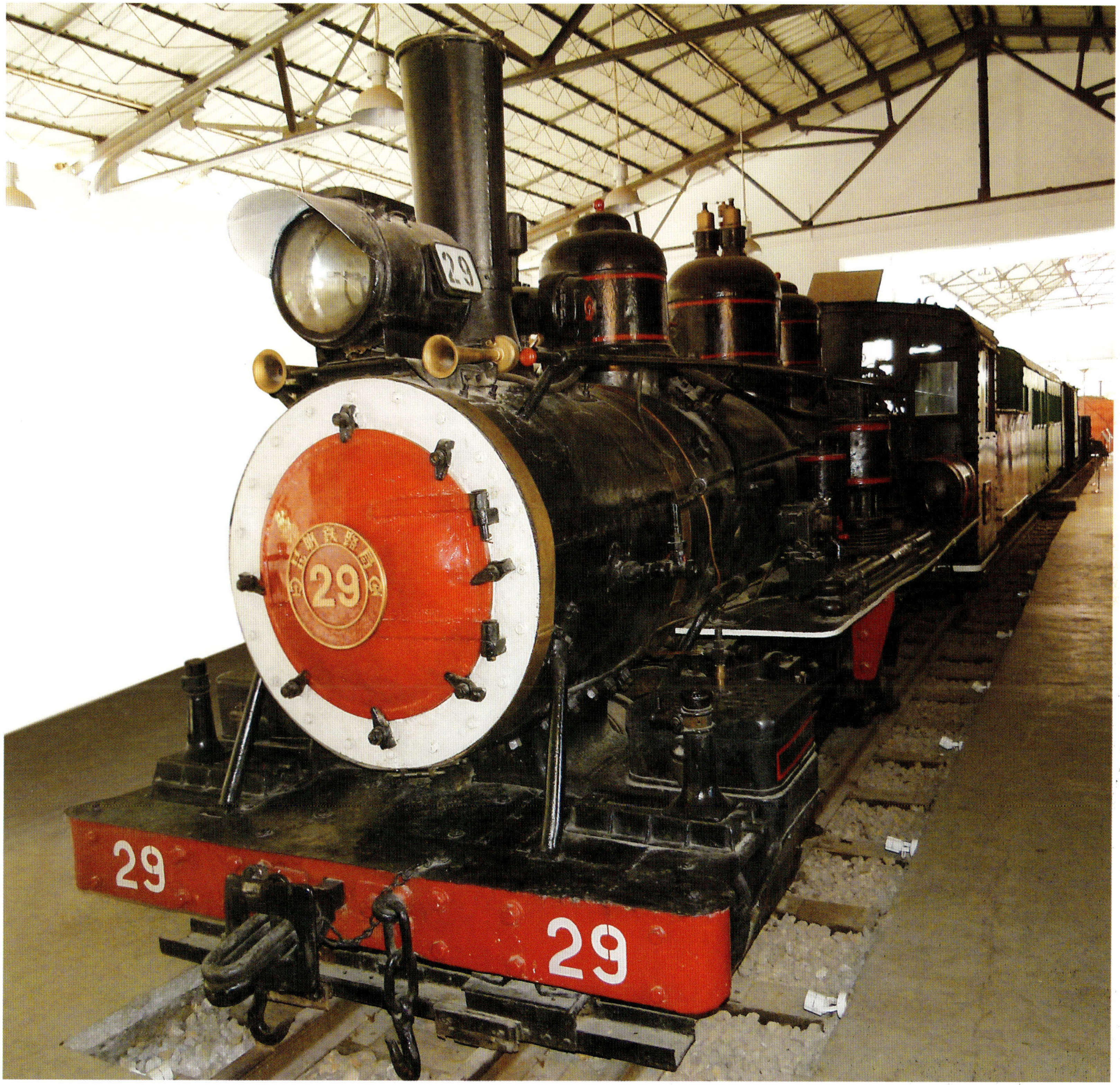
29
29
29
29

003 KD_{55}型米轨蒸汽机车（三级文物）

日本川崎造船所1897年制造的KD_{55}型蒸汽机车，车轴形排列方式1–4–0，轨距1000毫米，牵引力16370千克，构造速度50千米/小时，机车主车和煤水车整备质量98.24吨，储煤6吨，储水13吨，机车长16563毫米，宽2616毫米，高3813毫米。1958年至1985年服役于云南铁路。

KD_{55} Steam Locomotive for 1000mm Gauge（National Grade–three Cultural Relic）

The KD_{55} steam locomotive (axial model of 1-4-0) was made by Kawasaki Shipbuilding Plant of Japan in 1897. The gauge of the car is 1000mm with the traction modulus of 16370kg. Its design speed is 50km per hour with a total weight of 98.24 tons including the main car and coal & water carriage. It can store 6 tons of coal and 13 tons of water. The car is 16563mm long, 2616mm wide and 3813mm high. It was used in Yunnan railway from 1958 to 1985.

004 缅甸铁路赠送英国产蒸汽机车

这是一台英国蒸汽机车，是缅甸联邦铁路赠送中国铁路的赠品。机车长11米，宽2.57米，高3.35米，自重42吨,型号ST，车号774，轨距1米，车轴排列方式为1-3-2，制动方式为真空型，其煤箱和水柜与主车组合为一体。

该机车于1948年进入缅甸铁路运营，至2006年7月退役。2006年9月19日，缅甸联邦铁路将其作为外交互赠礼品，赠送原中国铁道部，后由原中国铁道部分配昆明铁路局所辖云南铁路博物馆收藏。

The British-made Steam Locomotive Presented by Myanmar Railways

This British-made steam locomotive is a gift to China Railways sent by Myanmar Railways. It is 11m long, 2.57m wide, 3.35m high with the deadweight of 42 tons. It is model ST and numbered 774. The gauge is one meter with the axial model of 1-3-2. It uses the vacuum brake. The coal tank and water container are integrated with the main carriage.

The train went into operation on Myanmar Railway in 1948 and stopped its service in July of 2006. On September 19th 2006, it was presented by Myanmar Railways to the Original Ministry of Railways of China as a diplomatic gift. Later, it was given by the Original Ministry of Railways of China to Yunnan Railway Museum for collection under the jurisdiction of the Kunming Railway Administration.

005 缅甸铁路赠送德国产旅游客车

这是一辆德国制造的铁路客车车辆，是缅甸联邦铁路赠送中国铁路的赠品。型号BTS，车号002，载客定员24人，车长11.1米，宽2.74米，高3.5米，自重14吨。车体为钢架木结构，除钢梁框架外，车厢为木地木墙板，车窗为木质百叶窗，乘客座位为木椅，内设卫生间和盥洗室。

该车辆于1966年进入缅甸铁路运营，至2006年7月退役。2006年9月19日缅甸联邦铁路将其作为外交互赠礼品，赠送原中国铁道部，后由原中国铁道部分配昆明铁路局所辖云南铁路博物馆收藏。

The German-made Tourist Passenger Carriage Presented by Myanmar Railways

This German-made tourist carriage is a gift to China Railways sent by Myanmar Railways. It is model BTS and numbered 002 with a fixed capacity of 24 passengers. It is 11.1m long, 2.74m wide, 3.5m high with deadweight of 14 tons. Its body is made of steel and wood. The frame is made of steel, while the carriage has wood floor and wall, wood blinds, and wood seats. Toilets and washrooms are available in the carriage.

The carriage went into operation on Myanmar Railway in 1966 and stopped its service in July of 2006. On September 19th 2006, it was presented by Myanmar Railways to the Original Ministry of Railways of China as a diplomatic gift. Later, it was given by the Original Ministry of Railways of China to Yunnan Railway Museum for collection under the jurisdiction of the Kunming Railway Administration.

006 寸轨木质客车（一级文物）

个碧石寸轨铁路上运营的三等客车，车号241，由中国汉口扬子工厂于1919年生产。

The Wooden Passenger Car for 600mm Gauge（National Grade-one Cultural Relic）

This car is a third-class passenger carriage running on Gejiu-Bisezhai-Shiping Railway. It is numbered 241 and manufactured by Yangzi Factory of Hankou, China in 1919.

007 10吨寸轨铁质棚车（一级文物）

该车由美国Koppel车厂于1930年生产，载重10吨，车号451。

The Iron-made Ten-ton Box Wagon for 600mm Gauge (National Grade-one Cultural Relic)

This wagon was made by Koppel works of the United States in 1930, numbered 451 and with a capacity of 10 tons.

008 10吨寸轨木质敞车（一级文物）

该车由美国Magor车厂于1924年制造，车号601。

The Ten-ton High Boarding Wagon for 600mm Gauge (National Grade-one Cultural Relic)

This car was produced by Magor works of the United States in 1924, numbered 601.

009 10吨寸轨木质平车（一级文物）

该车由中国汉口扬子工厂于1919年制造，车号701。

The Ten-ton Wooden Plain Car for 600mm Gauge (National Grade-one Cultural Relic)

This car was made by Yangzi works of Hankou, China, numbered 701.

010 10吨寸轨木质棚车（一级文物）

该车由法国Decauville车厂于1925年制造，车号402。

The Ten-ton Wooden Box Wagon for 600mm Gauge (National Grade-one Cultural Relic)

This wagon was made by Decauville works of France in 1925, numbered 402.

011 寸轨行李邮政车（一级文物）

该车由中国汉口扬子工厂于1919年制造，车号351。

The Luggage and Mail Van for 600mm Gauge (National Grade-one Cultural Relic)

This van was made by Yangzi works of Hankou, China in 1919, and numbered 351.

012 米轨木质客车（二级文物）

车号371、372，自重20吨，车辆长12.5米，宽2.8米，高3.8米。此类车辆由法国于1940年生产，1985年停用，可载客52人。

The Wooden Passenger Car with Hard Seats for 1000mm Gauge (National Grade-two Cultural Relic)

This car is numbered 371 and 372,with deadweight of 20 tons, length of 12.5 meters, width of 2.8 meters and height of 3.8 meters. This series of cars manufactured by France in 1940, with capacity of 52 passengers. It stopped its service in 1985.

013 10吨米轨木质棚车401号

此型号的车辆，由法国生产，是滇越铁路运营初期使用数量最多的载货棚车，载重10吨，1958年后淘汰停用，现国内存世的仅此一辆，价值珍贵。该车辆构造独特，车顶一端设有具有人性化的专供制动人员遮风避雨的“风雨篷”。

Ten-ton Wooden Box Wagon for 1000mm Gauge Numbered 401

With load of ten tons, this model of cars made by France was the most used cargo wagon at the beginning of operation of Yunnan-Vietnam Railway. It was obsolete and out of use in 1958. This wagon is the only one that still exists today, thus rare and precious. This car was uniquely designed that a humanized "shelter" was made on an end of carriage top to prevent brake staff from winds and rains.

019 准轨春城号动车组

动车长26.125米，宽3.014米，高4.134米，自重53.4吨；拖车长26.600米，宽3.104米，高4.134米，自重56.2吨。

该车由昆明铁路局与长春客车厂和株洲电力机车研究所联合研制。1999年举办中国昆明世界园艺博览会时，作为旅游列车开行于昆明—石林之间。春城号动车组是中国铁路早期探索制造高速动车组的先行者。云南铁路博物馆收藏展示其中的动车和拖车各一辆。

The 1435mm Gauge "Chunchenghao" CRH (China Railway High-speed) Train

This CRH train is 26.125 meters long, 3.014 meters wide, 4.134 meters high and weighs 53.4 tons; The trailer of it is 26.600 meters long, 3.104 meters wide, 4.134 meters high and weighs 56.2 tons.

This car was designed and manufactured by Kunming Railways Administration, Changchun Passenger Car Works and Zhuzhou Electric Locomotive Research Institute. This car ran between Kunming and Shilin as a travel car in 1999 when the Horticultural Expo of Kunming was opened. The "Chunchenghao" serves as a pioneer of early-stage CHR. A locomotive and a trailer of it are exhibited in Yunnan Railways Museum.

020 测量仪器的脚架和尺杆（三级文物）

年代：1901年　　产地：法国

Rack of Measuring Instruments and Sighting Rod (National Grade-three Cultural Relic)

Year: 1901　　Place of production: France

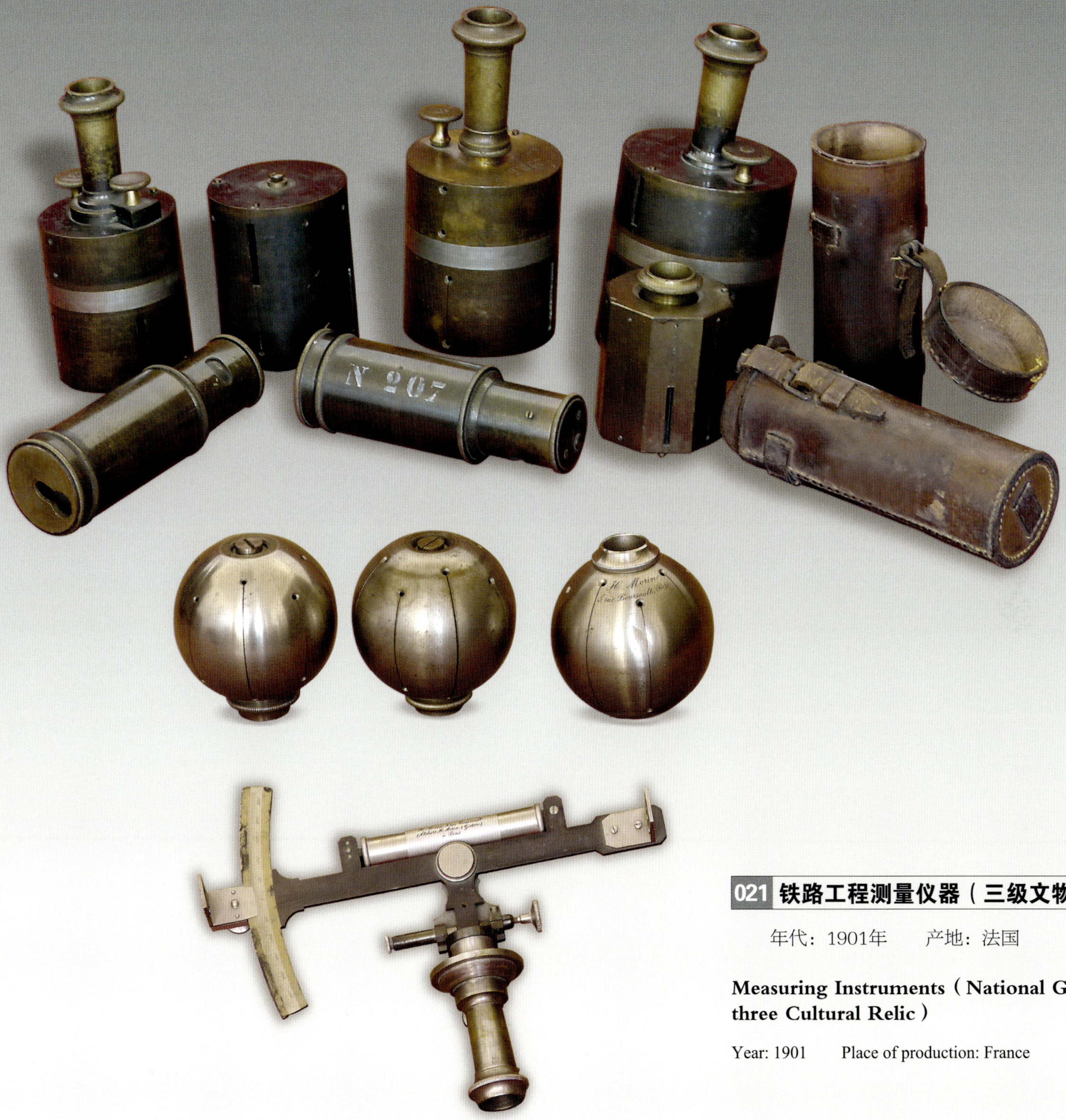

021 铁路工程测量仪器（三级文物）

年代：1901年　　产地：法国

Measuring Instruments（National Grade-three Cultural Relic）

Year: 1901　　Place of production: France

022 钢卷尺（三级文物）

年代：1901年　　产地：法国

Steel Measuring Tape（National Grade-three Cultural Relic）

Year: 1901　　Place of production: France

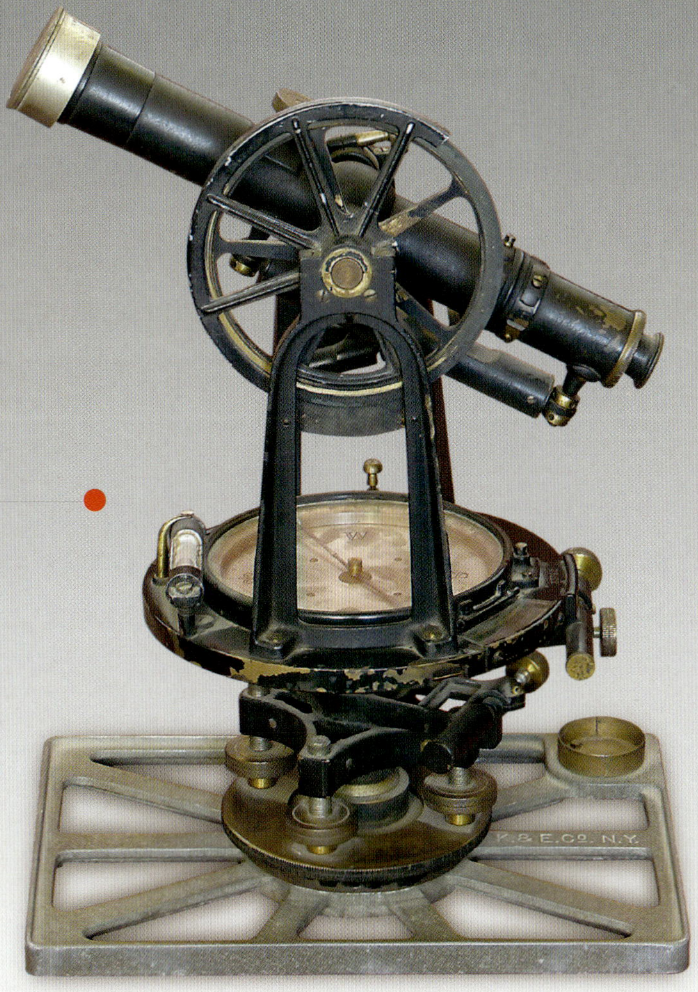

经纬仪是测量工作中的主要测角仪器，由望远镜、水平度盘、竖直度盘、水准器和基座组成。

023 经纬仪（二级文物）

年代：19世纪　产地：美国

Theodolite（National Grade-two Cultural Relic）

Year: 19th century　Place of production: U.S.A

024 莫林360度经纬仪（二级文物）

年代：1901年　　产地：法国

A H.Morin360° Theodolite（National Grade-two Cultural Relic）

Year: 1901　　Place of production: France

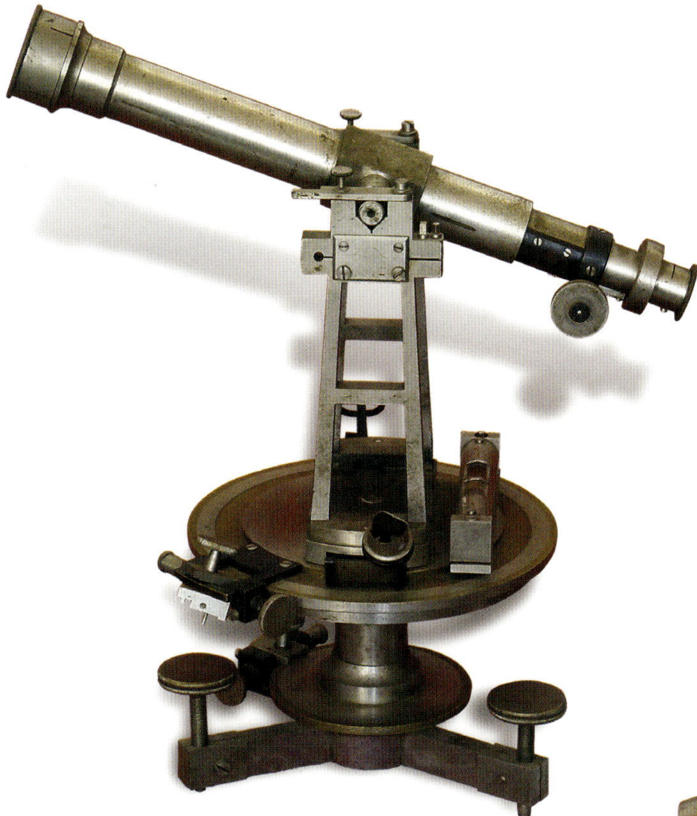

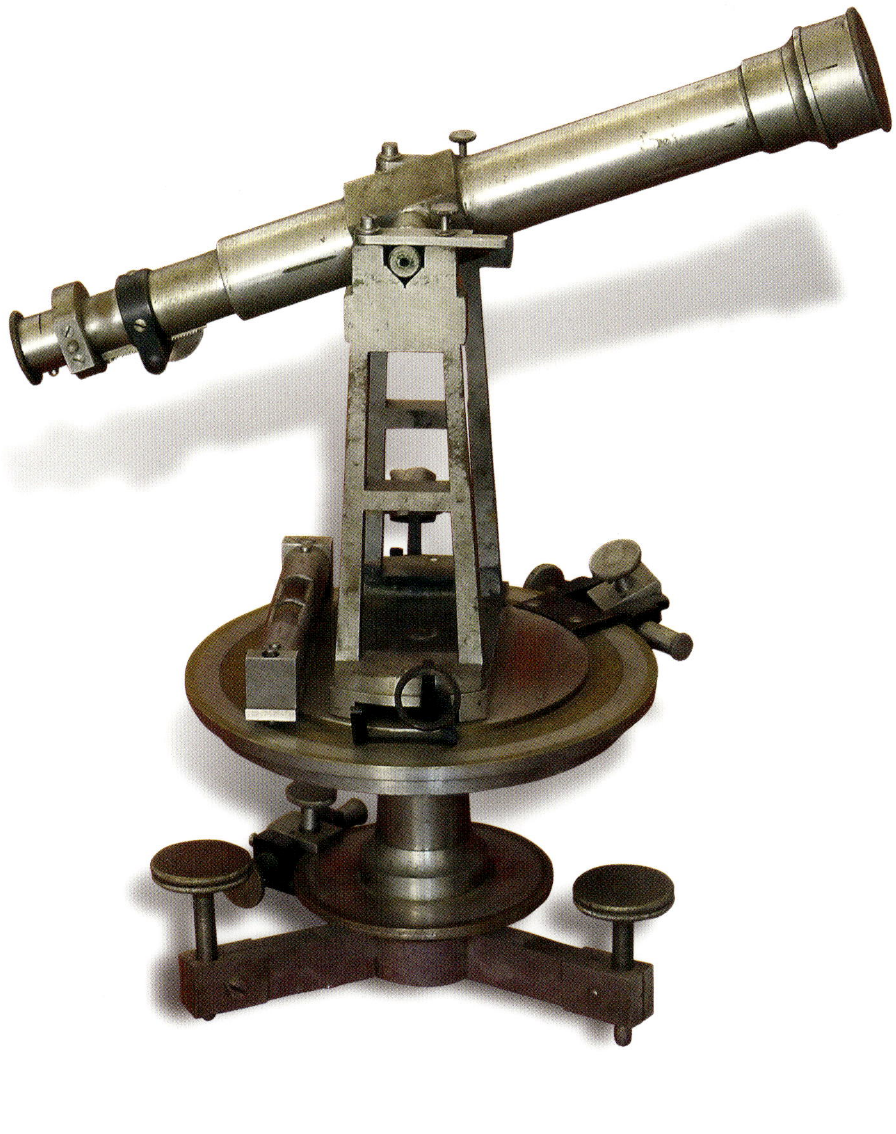

025 伯迪勒米400度经纬仪（三级文物）

年代：1901年　　产地：法国

A Berihelemy 400° Theodolite（National Grade-three Cultural Relic）

Year: 1901　　Place of production: France

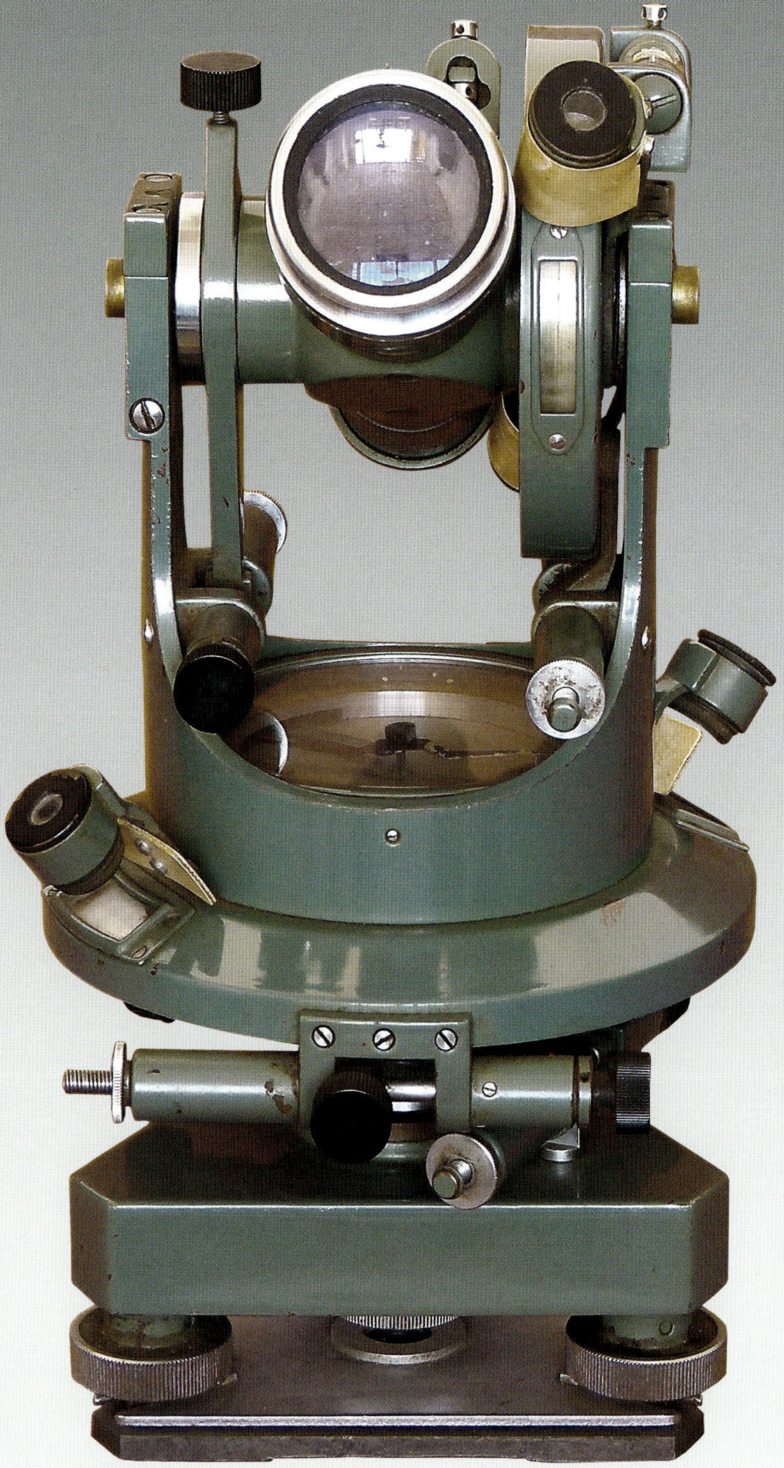

026 经纬仪

年代：1960年　　产地：中国上海

Theodolite

Year: 1960　　Place of production: Shanghai, China

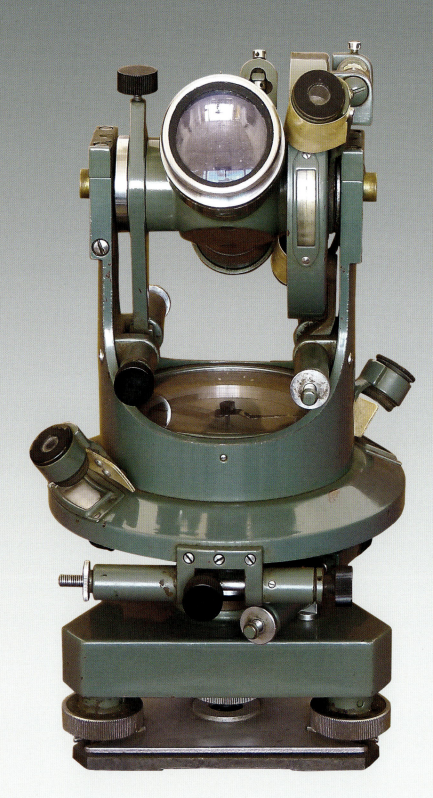

水平仪是利用重力现象测量微小角度的测量工具。玻璃管内装有黏滞系数小的酒精、乙醚等液体，但留有一个气泡，它随玻璃管倾斜而移动，从玻璃管上的刻度可以读出倾斜的角度。

027 水平仪（三级文物）

年代：1901年　　产地：法国

Gradienter（National Grade-three Cultural Relic）

Year: 1901　　Place of production: France

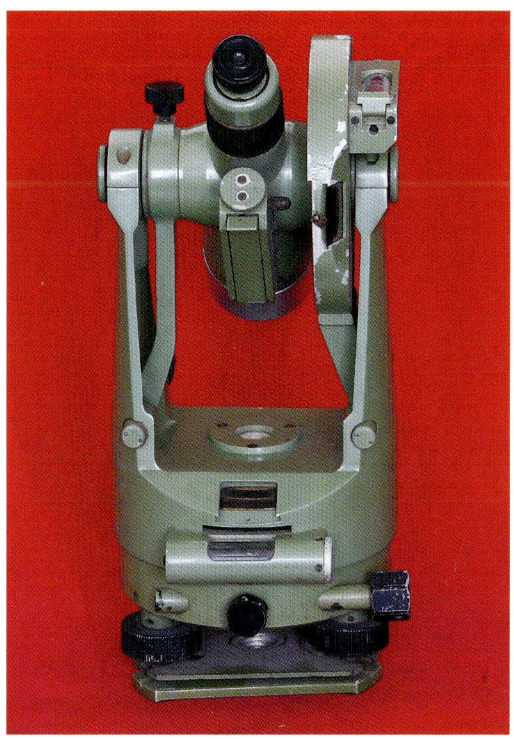

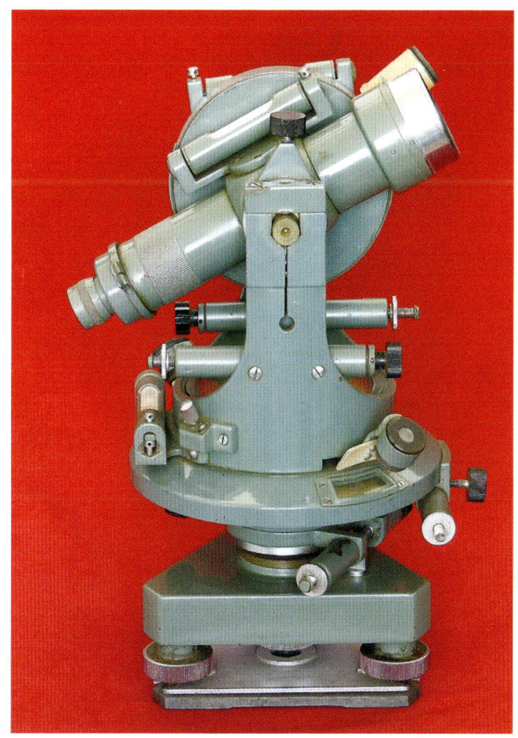

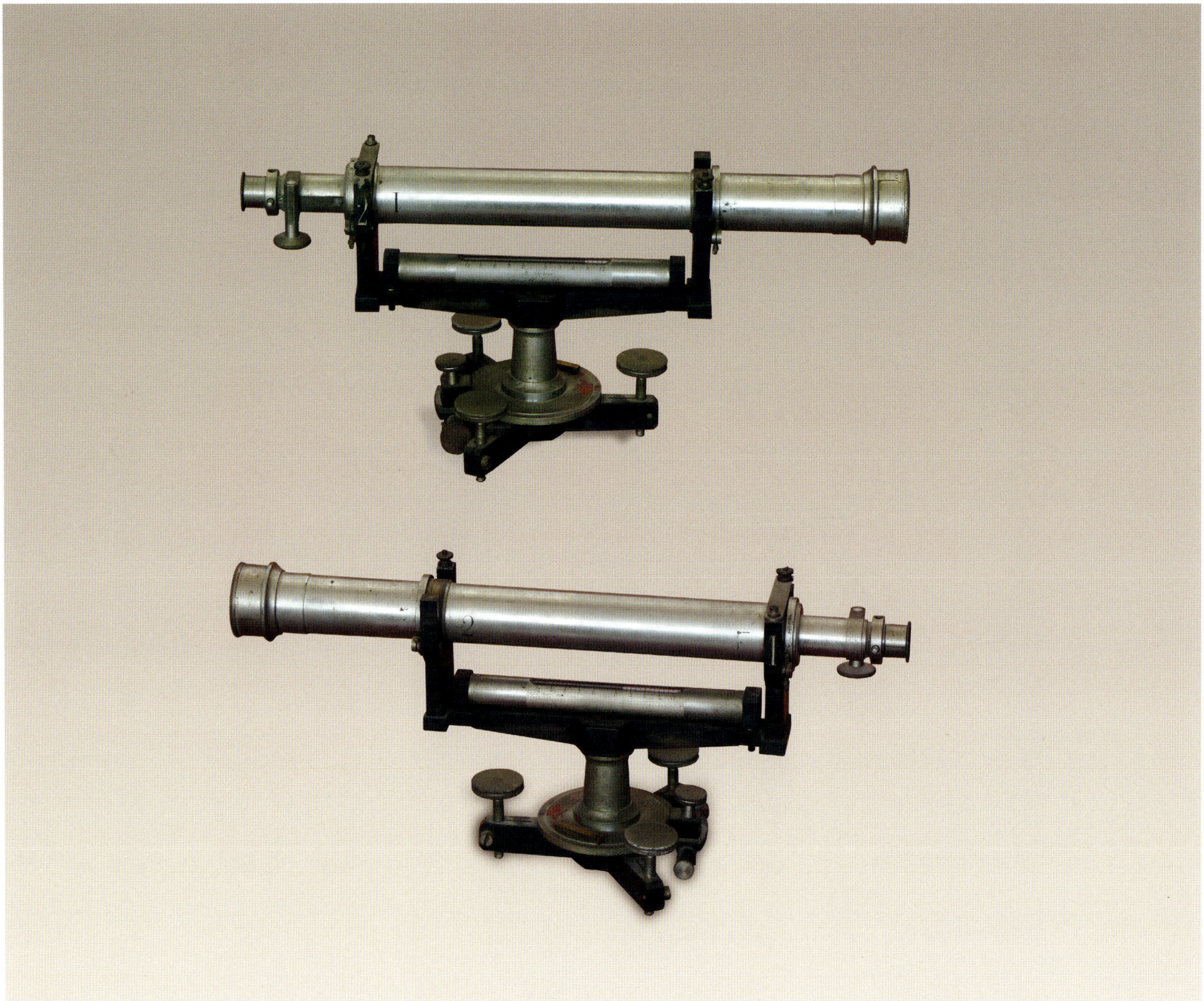

028 莫林水平仪（三级文物）

年代：1901年　　产地：法国

A H. Morin Gradienter（National Grade-three Cultural Relic）

Year: 1901　　Place of production: France

水准仪是测量高程的仪器，是建筑工程里提供高程基准的测设标高仪器。

029 水准仪（三级文物）

年代：19世纪　　产地：美国

Gradienter（National Grade-three Cultural Relic）

Year: 19th century　　Place of production: U.S.A

030 制图曲线板

年代：1950年　　产地：中国上海

Drawing Curve Board

Year: 1950　　Place of production: Shanghai, China

031 木质平板测量仪

The Wooden Flat Measuring Instrument

032 滇越铁路线路纵断面蓝图册（二级文物）

1901 ~ 1910年，法国工程师绘制。

Vertical Section Blueprints of the Railway Line of Yunnan–Vietnam Railway (National Grade–two Cultural Relic)

1901~1910, drawn by French engineers.

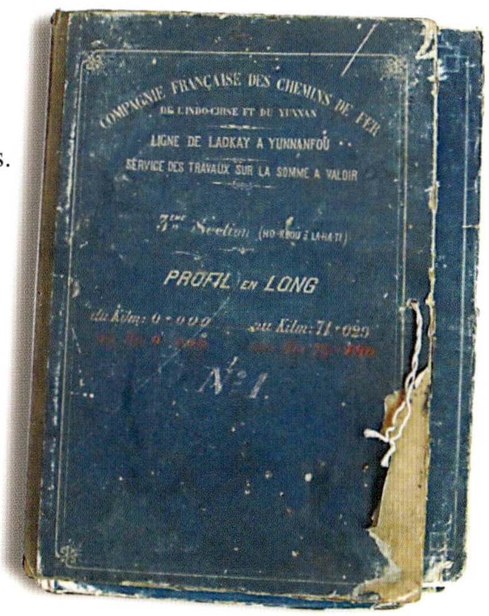

033 滇缅铁路平面剖面图（二级文物）

Flat Profile of Yunnan–Myanmar Railway (National Grade–two Cultural Relic)

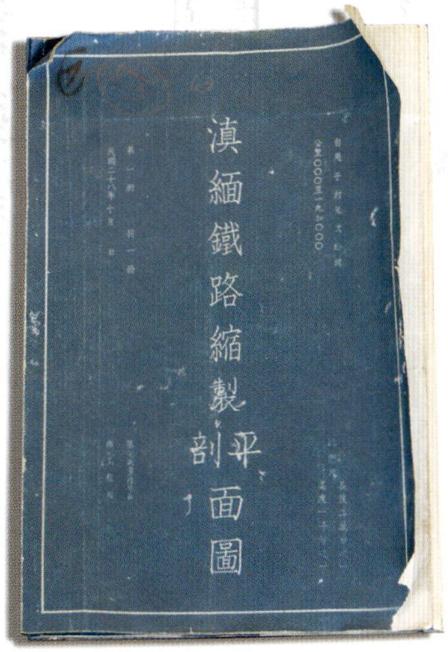

034 昆河线碧河段修复工程调查报告

Survey Report of Restoration Works of Bisezhai–Hekou Section on Kunming–Hekou Railway

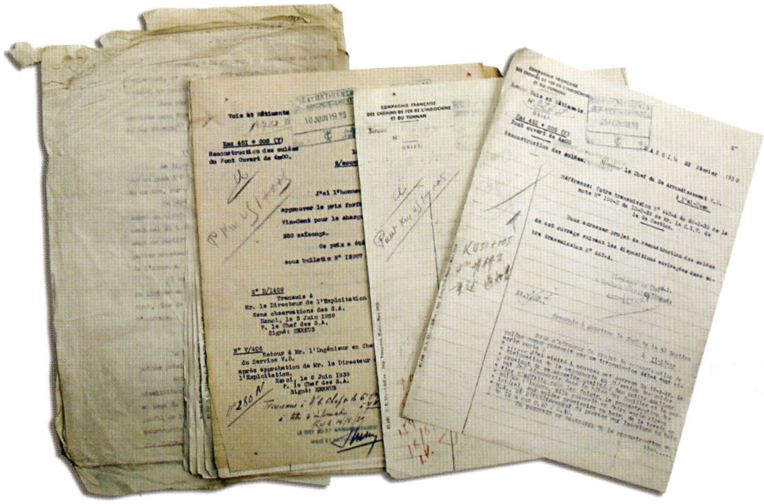

035 铁路设施检修设计图（三级文物）

1912～1939年，法国工程师绘制。

Overhaul and Design Drawing of Railway Equipment（National Grade-three Cultural Relic）

1912~1939, drawn by French engineers.

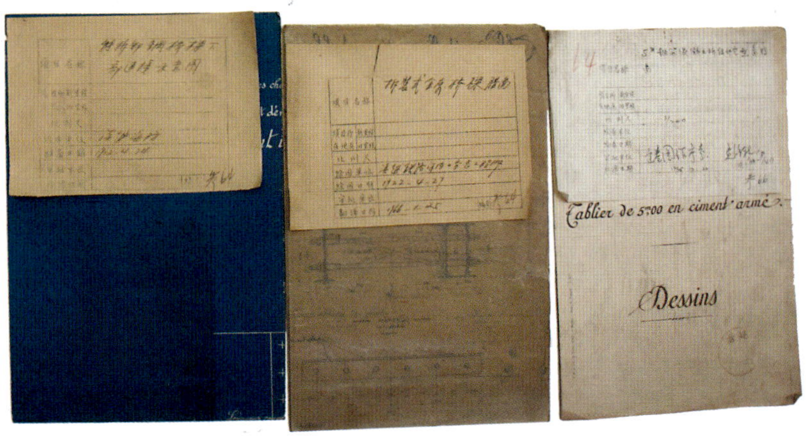

036 滇越铁路桥梁设计图（三级文物）

1901～1940年，法国工程师绘制。

Bridge Design Drawing of Yunnan-Vietnam Railway（National Grade-three Cultural Relic）

1901~1940, drawn by French engineers.

037 修建滇越铁路所用土地的地亩图

1903～1940年，法国工程师绘制。

Part of the Drawings of Requisitioned Land for Building Yunnan-Vietnam Railway

1903~1940, drawn by French engineers.

038 叙昆铁路建设标准图（三级文物）

1938年，中国川滇铁路公司绘制。

The Standard Construction Drawing of Yibin–Kunming Railway（National Grade–three Cultural Relic）

In 1938, drawn by Sichuan-Yunnan Railway Company.

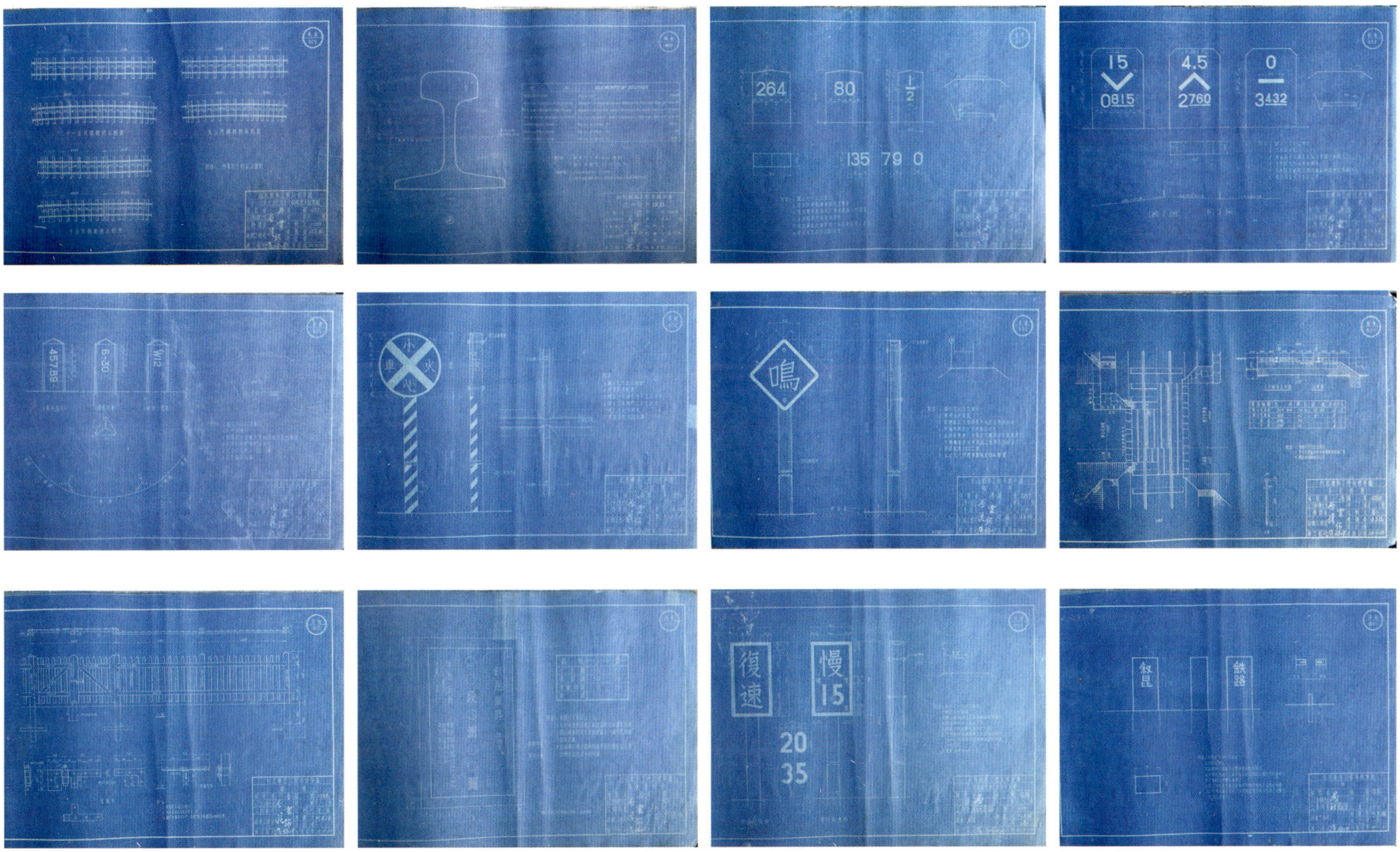

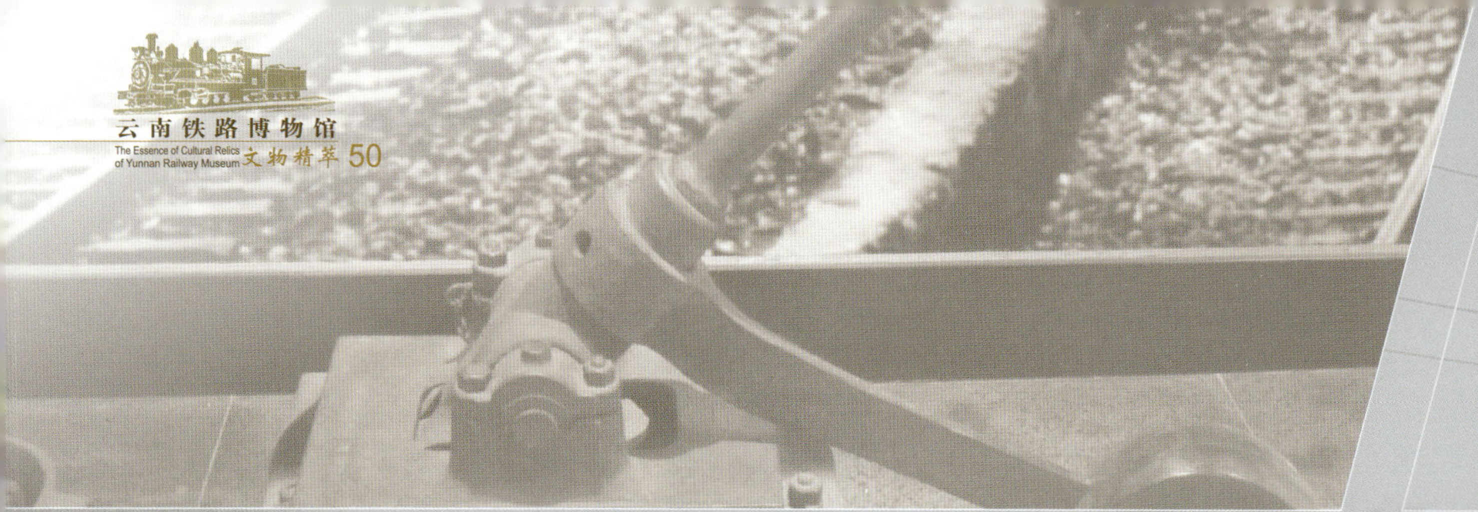

If locomotives and rolling stocks are musical notes of the movement, the railway tracks will be music stave. The early Yunnan railway was called "Universal Railway" due to its complex history. Rails sourcing from various countries, mixed specification models, and miscellaneous equipment accessories reflect the hard time foot printed by Yunnan railway.

The history information is preserved in steel rails shown with different standards from France, Germany, Britain, the United States, Russia and China. As a Chinese proverb states, "The journey of a thousand miles begins with a single step." Through these steel rails, you may hear symphonic variations sometimes low and deep but sometimes loud and sonorous, which play the movement of Yunnan railway with glanderous affections and in firm foot steps ahead.

第 3 章

Article third

线路设备

Railway Tracks

如果机车车辆是一曲乐章的音[illegible]就是标记音乐的线谱。由于历史的原因[illegible]号称“万国铁路”，来源国别多，规格型[illegible]，客观反映了云南铁路走过的艰辛岁月。

博物馆陈列的一组[illegible]德、英、美、俄和中国等国家规格大小不一的钢轨实物[illegible]着云南铁路百年发展的历史信息，从这些火车“千里[illegible]足下”的铁路钢轨，您也许能聆听到时而低沉、时而[illegible]变奏交响曲，那是云南铁路壮怀激烈、铿锵而行的历[illegible]

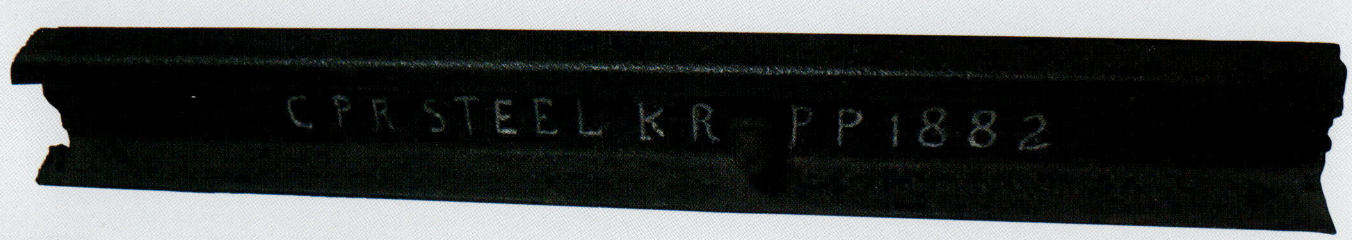

039 德国钢轨（25千克/米　三级文物）

年代：1882年　　生产：德国克虏伯公司

German Rail (25kg/m; National Grade-three Cultural Relic)

Year: 1882　　Producer: Krupp co., Ltd of German

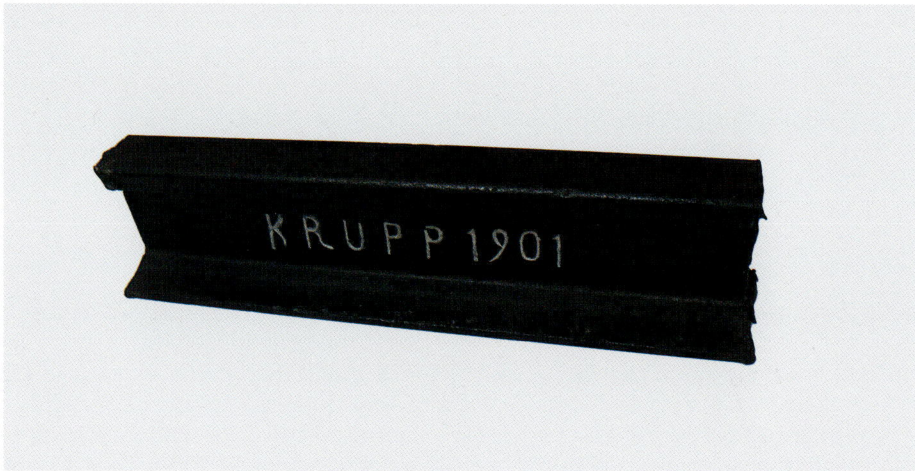

040 德国钢轨（30千克/米　三级文物）

年代：1901年　　生产：德国克虏伯公司

German Rail (30kg/m; National Grade-three Cultural Relic)

Year: 1901　　Producer: Krupp co., Ltd of German

041 德国钢轨（30千克/米　三级文物）

年代：1903年　　生产：德国克虏伯公司

German Rail (30kg/m; National Grade-three Cultural Relic)

Year: 1903　　Producer: Krupp co., Ltd of German

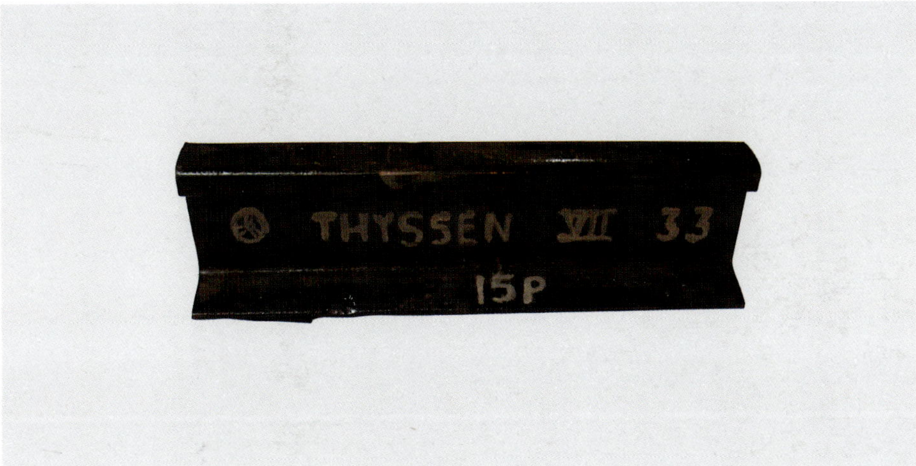

042 德国蒂森钢轨（三级文物）

年代：1910年　　产地：德国

"Thyssen " Rail of Germany (National Grade-three Cultural Relic)

Year: 1910　　Place of production: Germany

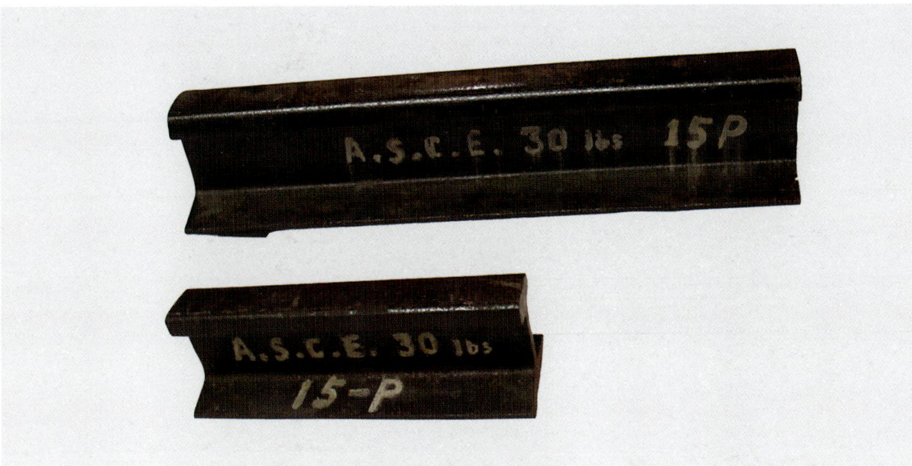

043 德国A.S.C.E钢轨（15千克/米　三级文物）

年代：1930年　　产地：德国

German A.S.C.E Rail (15kg/m; National Grade-three Cultural Relic)

Year: 1930　　Place of production: Germany

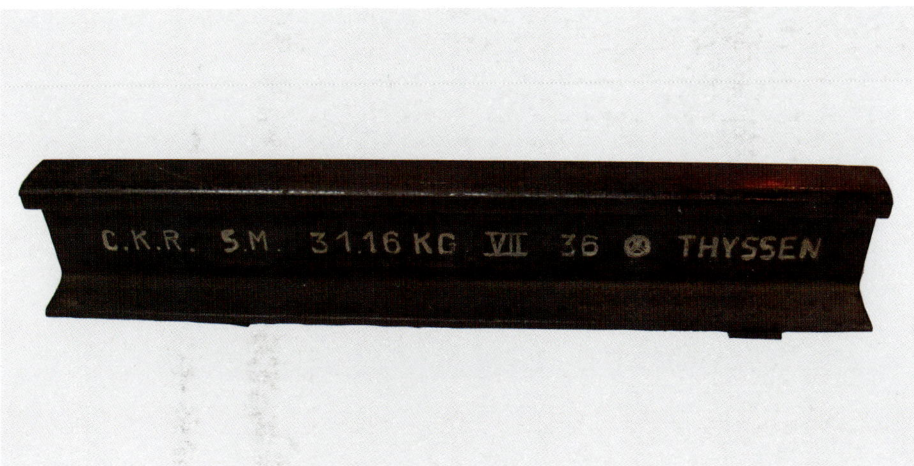

044 德国蒂森钢轨（31.16千克/米　三级文物）

年代：1936年　　产地：德国

"Thyssen " Rail of Germany (31.16kg/m; National Grade-three Cultural Relic)

Year: 1936　　Place of production: Germany

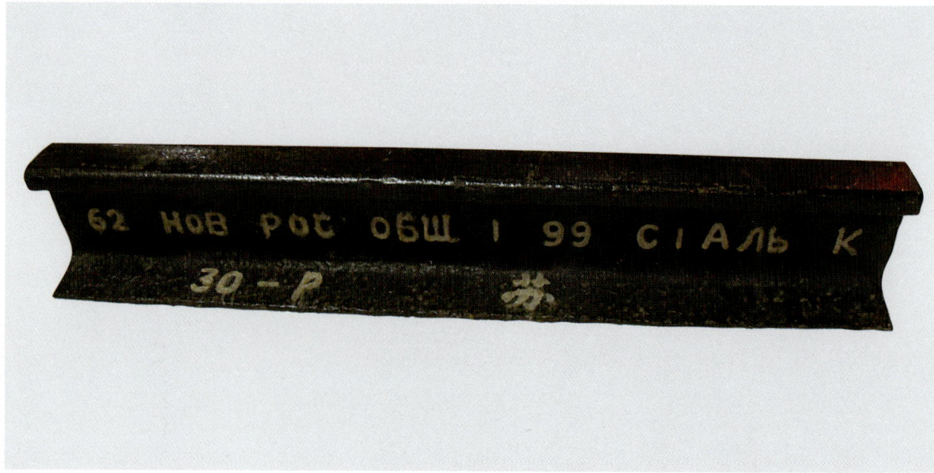

045 俄国钢轨（30千克/米　三级文物）

年代：1899年　　产地：俄国

Russian Rail（30kg/m; National Grade-three Cultural Relic）

Year: 1899　　Place of production: Russia

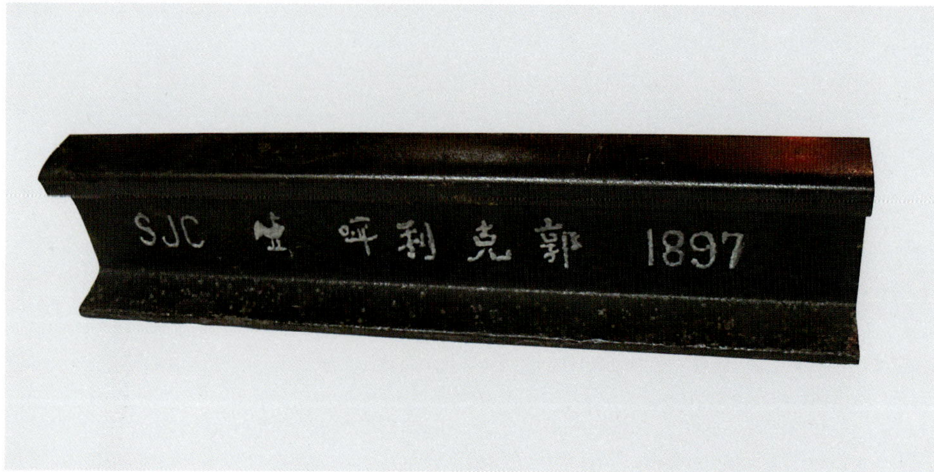

046 法国钢轨（32千克/米　三级文物）

年代：1897年　　产地：法国

French Rail（32kg/m; National Grade-three Cultural Relic）

Year: 1897　　Place of production: France

047 法国N-E-BB钢轨（25千克/米　三级文物）

年代：1904年　　产地：法国

French N-E-BB Rail（25kg/m; National Grade-three Cultural Relic）

Year: 1904　　Place of production: France

048 法国钢轨（25千克/米　三级文物）

年代：1904年　　生产：法国托马斯热福公司

French Rail（25kg/m; National Grade-three Cultural Relic）

Year: 1904　　Producer: B-Th-JOEUF co., Ltd of France

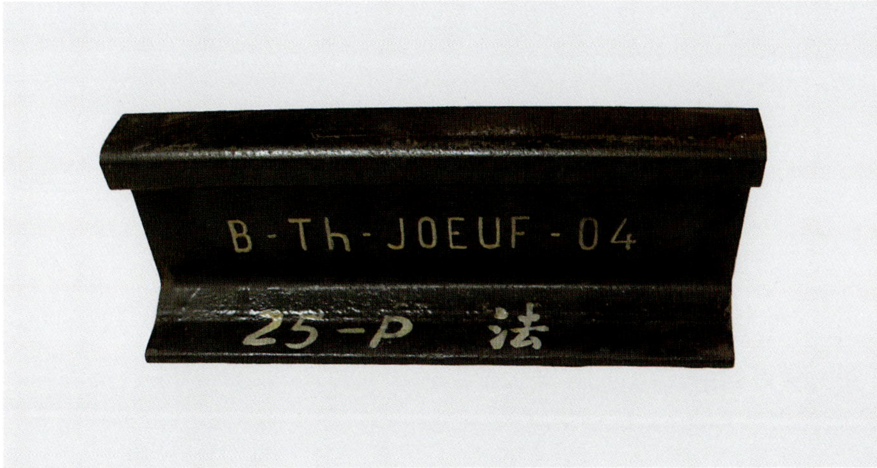

049 法国钢轨（30千克/米　三级文物）

年代：1907年　　生产：法国乌格莱公司

French Rail（30kg/m; National Grade-three Cultural Relic）

Year: 1907　　Producer: Ougree co., Ltd of France

050 法国钢轨（40千克/米　三级文物）

年代：1910年　　生产：法国hoesch公司

French Rail（40kg/m; National Grade-three Cultural Relic）

Year: 1910　　Producer: Hoesch co., Ltd of France

051 法国钢轨（38千克/米　三级文物）

年代：1927年　　生产：法国公司

French Rail（38kg/m; National Grade-three Cultural Relic）

Year: 1927　　Producer: A.R.A co., Ltd of France

052 法国钢轨（16千克/米　三级文物）

年代：1935年　　生产：法国米歇尔公司

French Rail（16kg/m; National Grade-three Cultural Relic）

Year: 1935　　Producer: Micheville co., Ltd of France

053 法国钢轨（43千克/米　三级文物）

年代：1934年
生产：法国平波公司

French Rail（43kg/m; National Grade-three Cultural Relic）

Year: 1934
Producer: Poht Talbot co., Ltd of France

054 法国TUNC-RU钢轨（16千克/米　三级文物）

年代：1936年　　产地：法国

French TUNC-RU Rail（16kg/m; National Grade-three Cultural Relic）

Year: 1936　　Place of production: France

055 法国钢轨（32千克/米　三级文物）

年代：1937年　　生产：法国波洪公司

French Rail（32kg/m; National Grade-three Cultural Relic）

Year: 1937　　Producer: BOHCKR co., Ltd of France

056 法国钢轨（33.48千克/米　三级文物）

年代：1937年　　生产：法国STUMM公司

French Rail（33.48kg/m; National Grade-three Cultural Relic）

Year: 1937　　Producer: STUMM co., Ltd of France

057 中东铁路钢轨

中东铁路(或东清铁路)是沙皇俄国在中国东北修建的铁路。К.В.Ж.Д是俄文“中国东方铁路”的缩写。MARYLAND表示钢轨为美国马里兰州生产。1900为钢轨生产年份1900年。

Rail Adopted By Chinese Eastern Railway

Chinese Eastern Railway (or Dongqing Railway) was built by Russia in Northeast of China. “К.В.Ж.Д”is the abbreviation of Chinese Eastern Railway (or Dongqing Railway) in Russian. “MARYLAND” demonstrates that the rail was produced in Maryland USA. “1900” refers to the year when the rail was made.

058 美国伊利诺伊钢轨

年代：1915年　产地：美国伊利诺伊州

Illinois Rail, U.S.A

Year: 1915　Place of production: Illinois U.S.A

059 中国汉阳铁厂钢轨

年代：1902（清朝）　产地：中国汉阳

Rail Made in Hanyang Ironworks of China

Year: 1902　Place of production: Hanyang, China

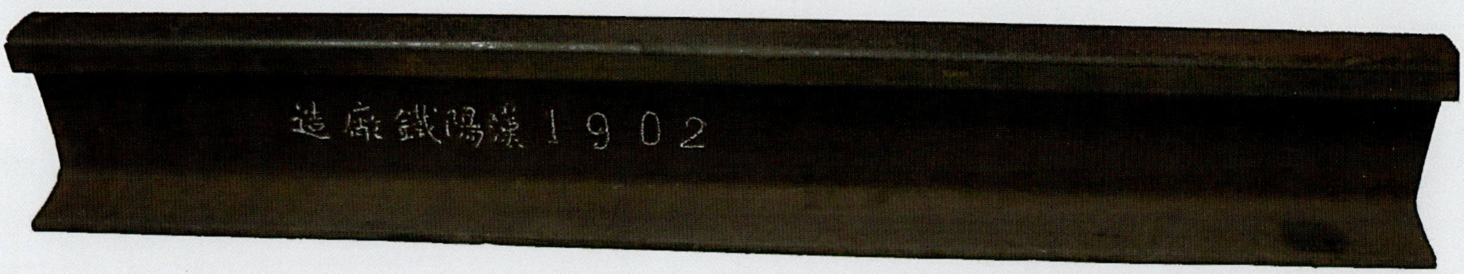

060 中国汉阳铁厂钢轨

年代：1903（清朝） 产地：中国汉阳

Rail Made in Hanyang Ironworks of China

Year: 1903 Place of production: Hanyang, China

061 中国汉阳钢铁厂钢轨

年代：1907（清朝） 产地：中国汉阳

Rail Made in Hanyang Ironworks of China

Year: 1907 Place of production: Hanyang, China

062 中国汉阳钢铁厂钢轨

年代：1908（清朝） 产地：中国汉阳

Rail Made in Hanyang Ironworks of China

Year: 1908 Place of production: Hanyang, China

063 中国汉阳钢铁厂钢轨

年代：1910（清朝）
产地：中国汉阳

Rail Made in Hanyang Ironworks of China

Year: 1910　　Place of production: Hanyang, China

064 中国汉阳钢铁厂钢轨

年代：1913（民国时期）
产地：中国汉阳

Rail Made in Hanyang Ironworks of China

Year: 1913　　Place of production: Hanyang, China

065 加拿大安大略钢轨

年代：1932年　　产地：加拿大安大略省

Algoma Rail, Canada

Year: 1932　　Place of production: Algoma, Canada

066 重庆钢铁厂钢轨

Rail Made in Chongqing of China

067 鞍山钢铁厂钢轨

Rail Made in Anshan of China

068 武汉钢铁厂钢轨

Rail Made in Wuhan of China

069 中华人民共和国出口钢轨（坦赞铁路采用）

年代：1971年　　产地：中国武汉

Rail Exported from the People's Republic of China (Rail Adopted by Tanzania-Zambia Railway)

Year: 1971　　Place of production: Wuhan, China

070 美国马里兰州钢轨

年代：1899年　　产地：美国马里兰产地

Maryland Rail, U.S.A

Year: 1899　　Place of production: Maryland, U.S.A

071 钢枕

年代：1931年　　产地：法国

Steel Sleeper

Year: 1931　　Place of production: France

钢轨连接夹板是一种用于钢轨与钢轨之间使用的连接紧固件。

072 钢轨连接夹板

Fishplate

073 钢轨连接夹板

Fishplate

074 钢轨连接夹板

Fishplate

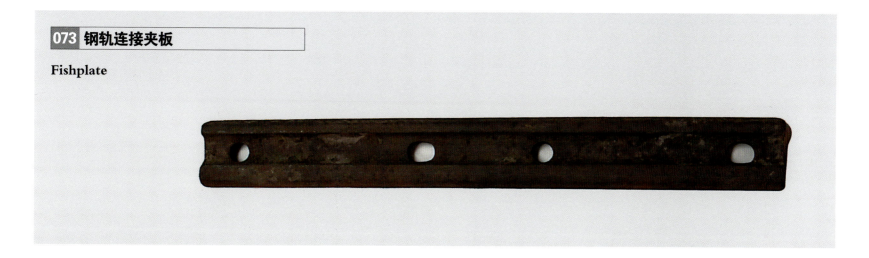

轨道尺是用于测量铁路线两股钢轨间的轨距、水平度以及超高等的专用计量器具。

075 铁质三角轨道尺

年代：1910年　　产地：法国

Triangle Track Gauge

Year: 1910　　Place of production: France

076 铁质轨道尺

年代：1910年　　产地：法国

Steel Gauge Measure

Year: 1910　　Place of production: France

077 木质轨道尺

年代：1960年　　产地：中国苏州

Wooden Gauge Measure

Year: 1960　　Place of production: Suzhou,China

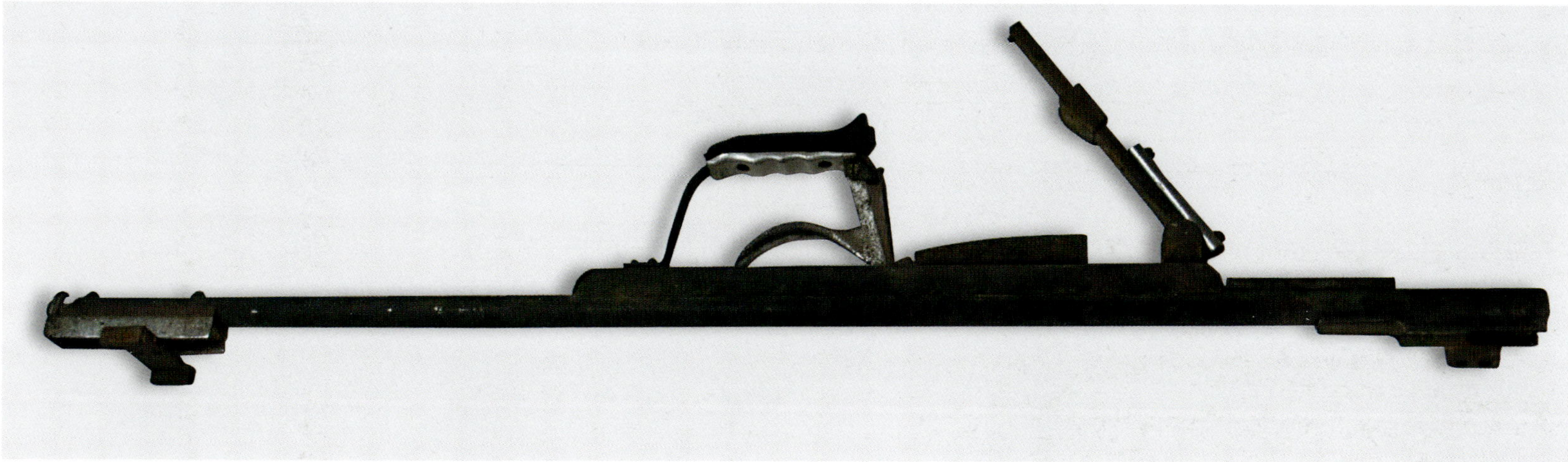

078 铁质轨道尺

年代：1910年　　产地：法国

Steel Gauge Measure

Year: 1910　　Place of production: France

079 铁质轨道尺

年代：1977年　　产地：中国

Steel Gauge Measure

Year: 1977　　Place of production: China

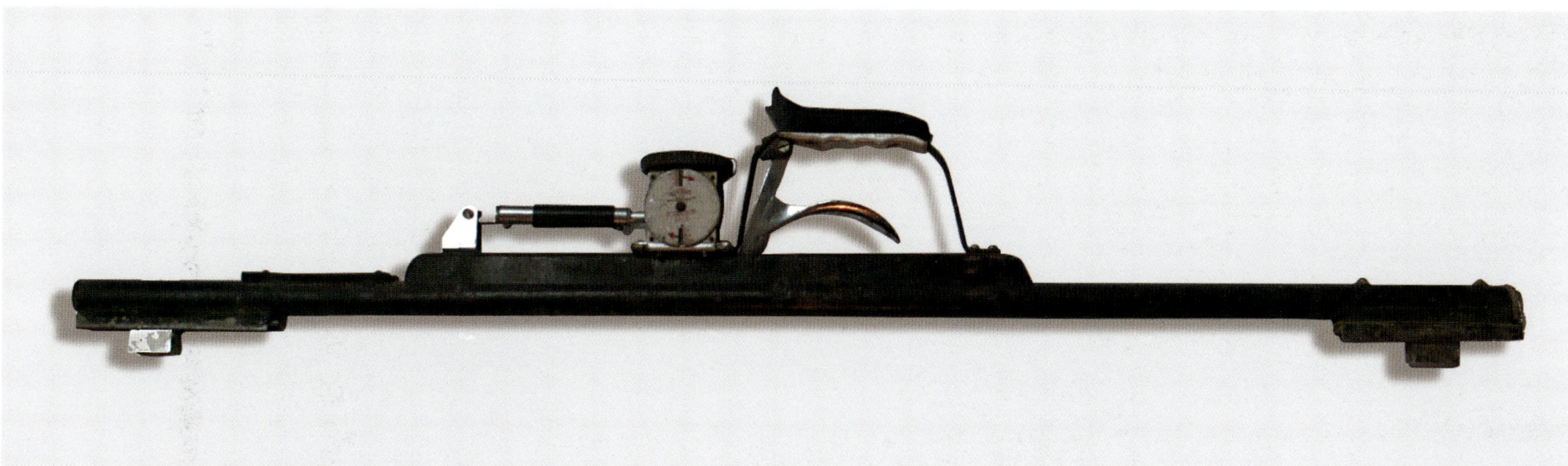

钢轨磨耗测量仪用于测量铁路运营线路钢轨的垂直磨耗和侧面磨耗，包括定位装置和测量装置。其结构简单，测量数据直观、准确，具有上、下道迅速，操作人员安全，重量轻，随身携带方便的特点。

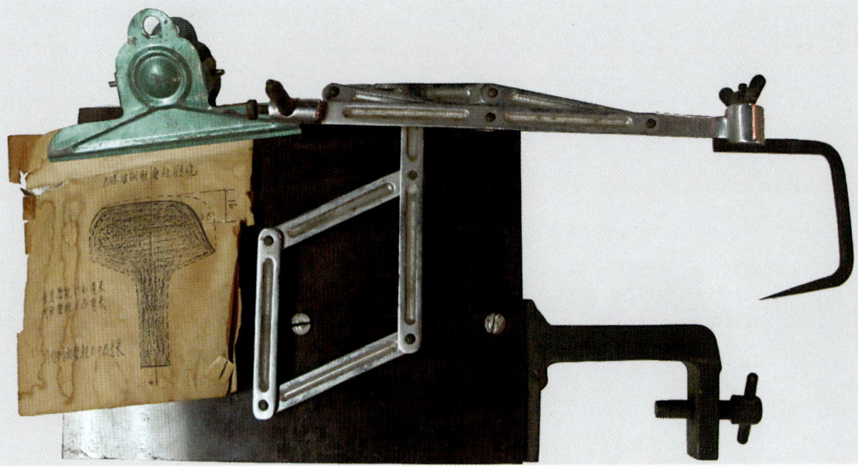

080 钢轨磨耗测量仪

年代：1960年　　产地：中国

A Tester of Rail Wear and Tear

Year: 1960　　Place of production: China

081 钢轨涂油器

年代：1961年　　产地：中国

Rail Lubricator

Year: 1961　　Place of production: China

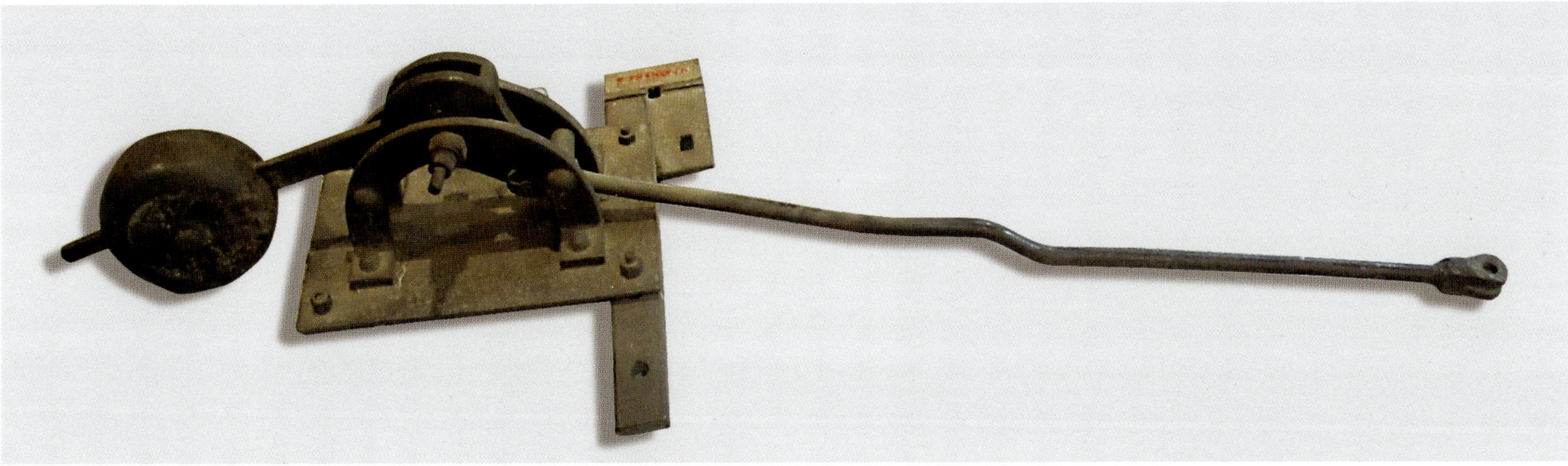

082 寸轨道岔转辙器（三级文物）

年代：1915年　　产地：法国

The Switch for 600mm Gauge Railway (National Grade-three Cultural Relic)

Year: 1915　　Place of production: France

道岔转辙器是车站铁路股道转换设备。

083 米轨道岔转辙器（三级文物）

年代：1902年　　产地：法国

The Switch for 1000mm Gauge Railway (National Grade-three Cultural Relic)

Year: 1902　　Place of production: France

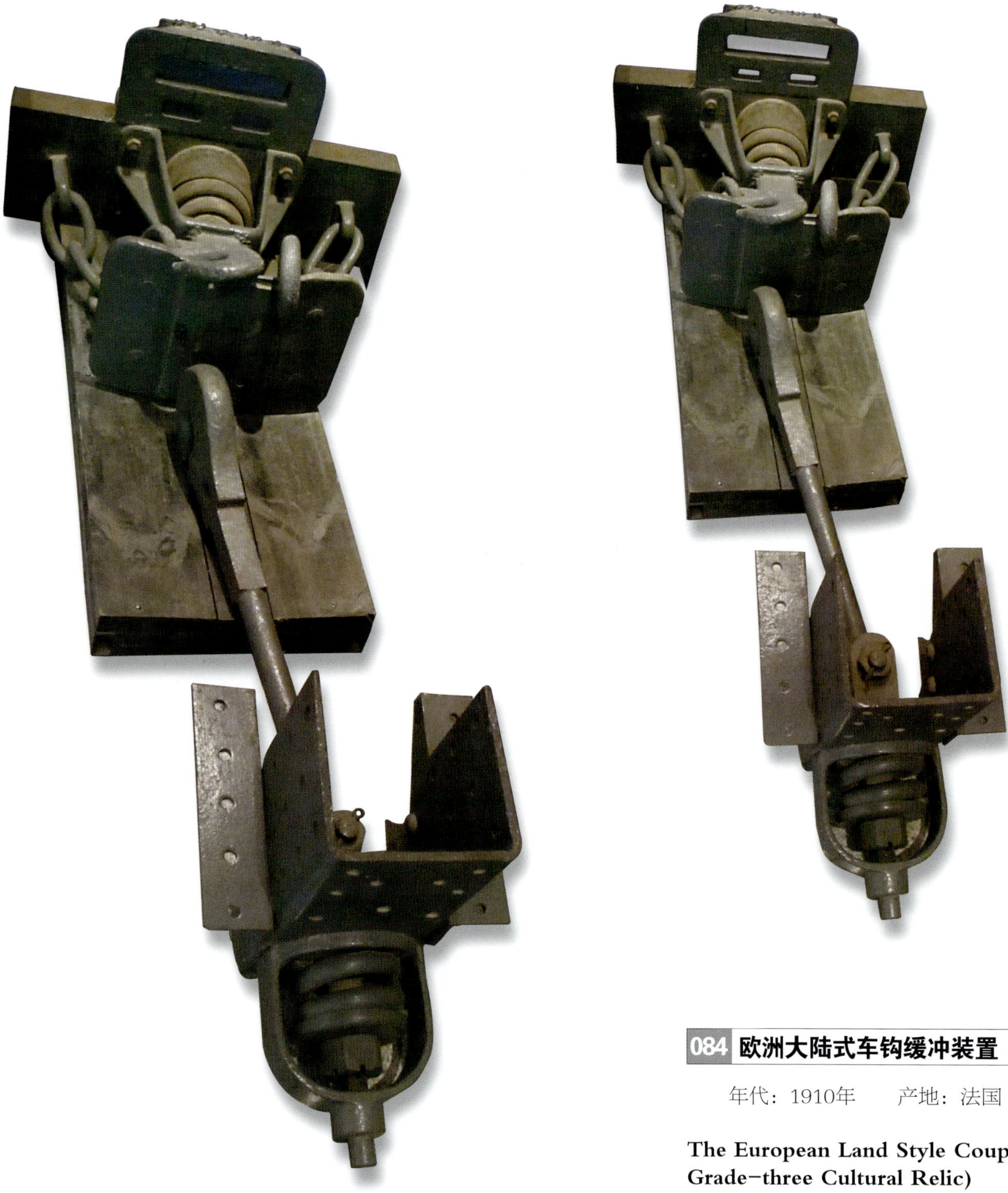

084 欧洲大陆式车钩缓冲装置（三级文物）

年代：1910年　　产地：法国

The European Land Style Coupler (National Grade-three Cultural Relic)

Year: 1910　　Place of production: France

铁路轨距
"Railway Gauge" means the distance between the two rails of a railway or between the wheels of a train. In China, there were many different gauges: the standard gauge (1435mm); broad gauge (more than 1435mm such as 1524mm); narrow gauge (less than 1435mm including 1067 mm, 1000mm, 762mm, 610mm, 600mm, etc).
寸轨钢轨和木枕
轨距：600毫米
规格：15千克/米
枕木材质：黑木
Rail and the wooden sleeper of 600mm gauge railway
The specification of weight of rail is 15kg per meter
The sleeper is made of hard wood
米轨钢轨和钢枕
轨距：1000毫米
规格：25千克/米
钢枕重量：36千克/块
Rail of 1000mm gauge railway and steel sleeper
The specification of weight of a rail is 25kg per meter
A piece of steel sleeper is 36kg
标准轨钢轨和轨枕
轨距：1435毫米
规格：60千克/米
The standard gauge is 1435mm.
A rail of standard gauge railway is 60kg per meter
The sleepers are made of wood and reinforced concrete

085 寸轨、米轨、准轨（标本）

因历史原因，云南铁路轨距多样，600毫米轨距、1000毫米轨距以及1435毫米标准轨距并存运营，在中国铁路运营史上别具一格。

Three Types of Gauges（600mm gauge、1000mm gauge and 1435mm gauge）

Due to its complex history, Yunnan railways cover various track gauges. The existence of three types of gauges including 600mm gauge, 1000mm gauge and 1435mm gauge is unique in the operation history of Chinese railways.

第4章

Article fourth

通信信号

Communications and Signals

通信和信号，是铁路运输的“千里眼”和“顺风耳”。看信号发车，拍电报联系，用电话调度；红蓝黄三色灯旗，代表不同的联系方式；报站钟、铜号角、报警响墩，表述特定的铁路语言；路签、路票、闭塞机，办理来来往往的行车通道；德国西门子、瑞典爱立信等世界名牌的电话机百十年前就服役在云南铁路的深山小站，这些当时的高科技在铁路员工手上仅仅是每天工作中使用的普通工具。

Communications and signals help the railway clairvoyant and clairaudient. We start trains only when signals shine, keep in contact by telegrams, and make schedules via telephones. Different meanings are stated in red, blue and yellow light flags. Unique railway languages are interpreted by station bells, copper horns and alarm torpedoes. Vehicles come and go across train staffs and block instruments. World renowned telephones with band of Siemens, Ericson etc. were in use in stations of remote mountains. To workers on the railway, high technologies of that day were merely common tools for their daily work.

086 铜钟

车站使用的老式报站钟，提醒旅客列车出发或到达。

年代：1920年　　产地：中国

Copper bells

An old stop announcer in station, reminding passengers of setting out or arrival.

Year: 1920　　Place of production: China

087 大五枚磁石电话机

年代：1930年

生产：中国国际电话公司

Telephone Made of 5 Big Magnets

Year: 1930

Producer: International Telephone Company of China

088 爱立信调度电话机

年代：1940年

产地：瑞典

Ericsson Magnet Telephone

Year: 1940

Place of production: Sweden

089 民国时期的磁石电话

Magnet Telephone Used During the Reign of Republic of China

090 手摇磁石电话

年代：1960年
生产：中国中天电机厂

The Hand-shaking Magnet Telephone

Year: 1960　　Producer: China

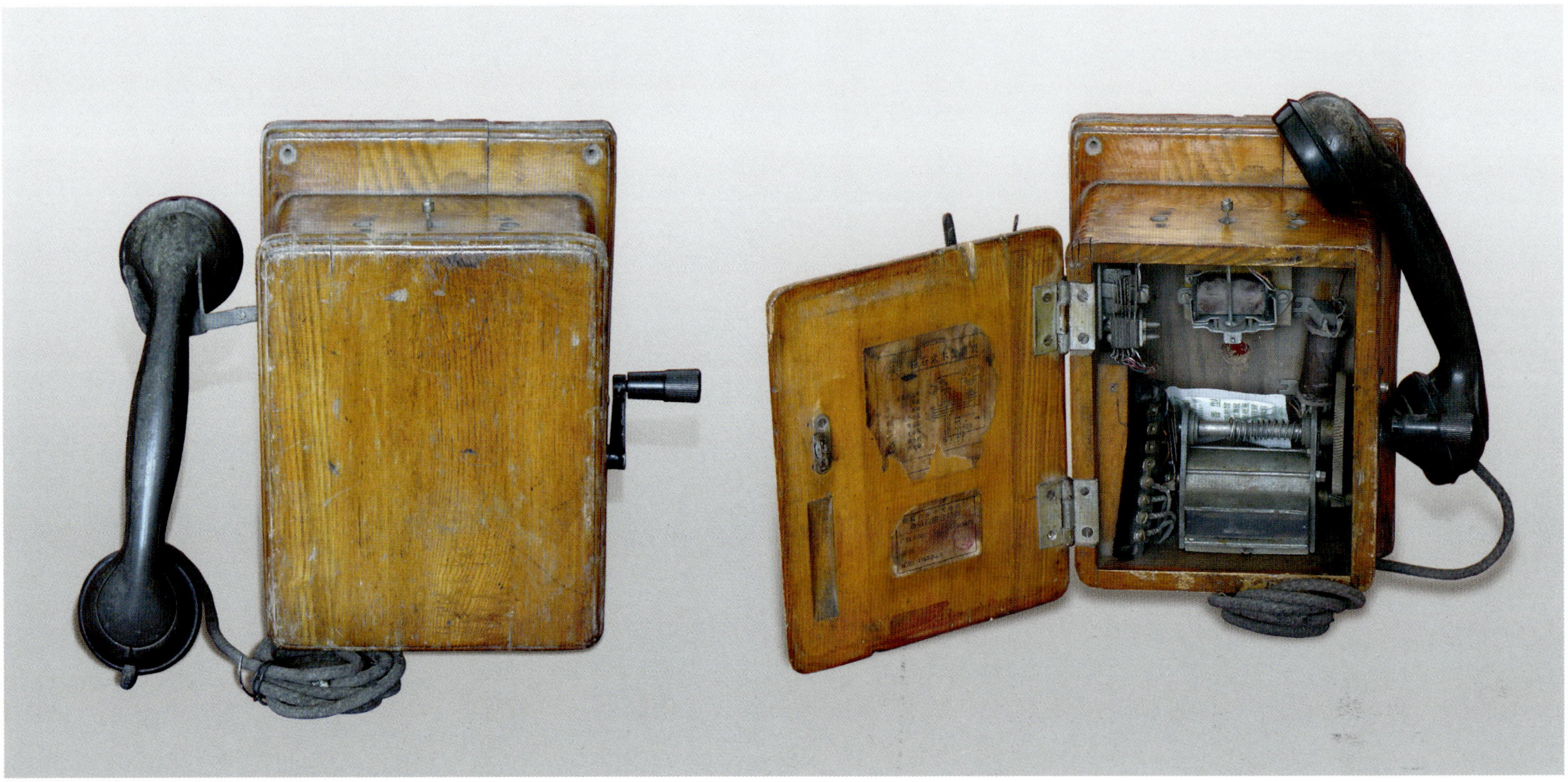

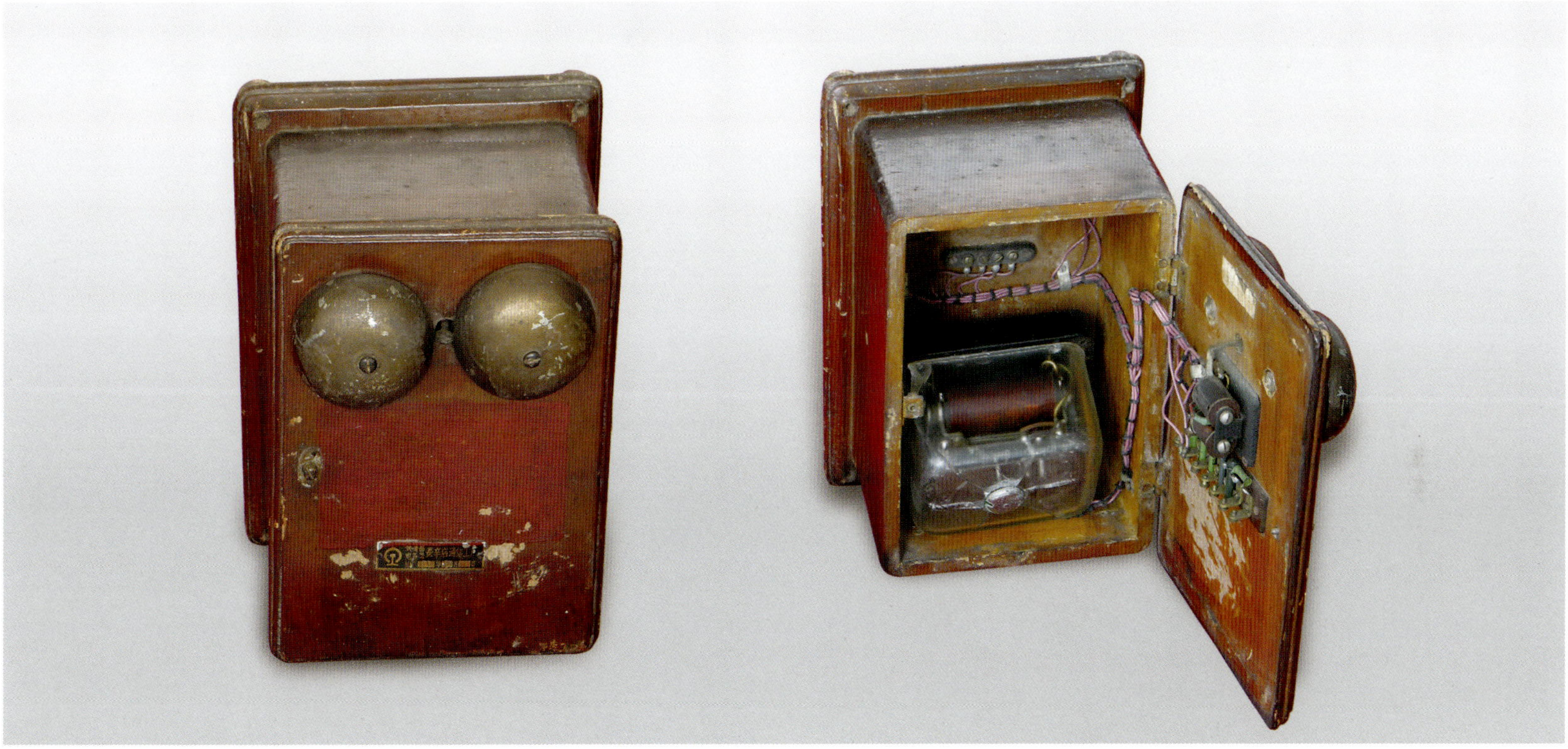

091 大五枚电话机

年代：1960年

生产：中国长辛店通信工厂

Telephone Made of 5 Big Magnets

Year: 1960　　Producer: China

092 电话小交换机

年代：1964年

产地：中国北京

A Small Switchboard

Year: 1964　　Place of production: Beijing, China

093 开甲9–1电话

生产：国营南京有线电厂

Kaijia 9–1 Telephone

Producer: Nanjing, China

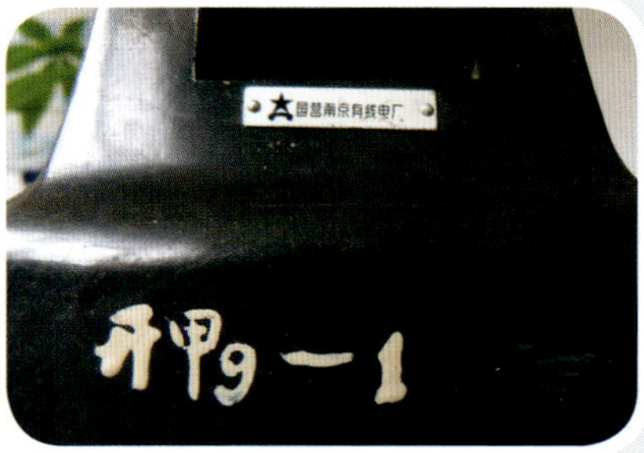

094 XD79携带电话机

XD79 Portable Telephone

095 便携式手摇电话机

年代：1970年　　产地：中国南京

Portable Hand-shaking Telephone

Year: 1970　　Place of production: Nanjing, China

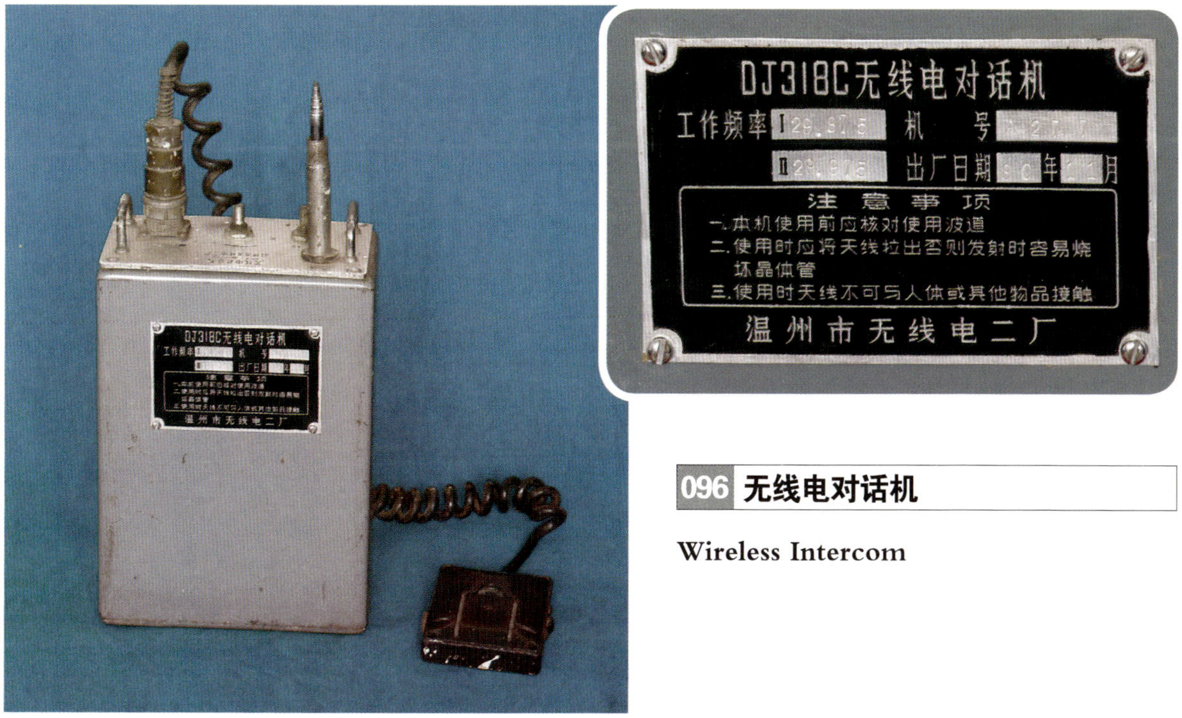

096 无线电对话机

Wireless Intercom

电话选别器用于老式磁石电话的号码选择和识别

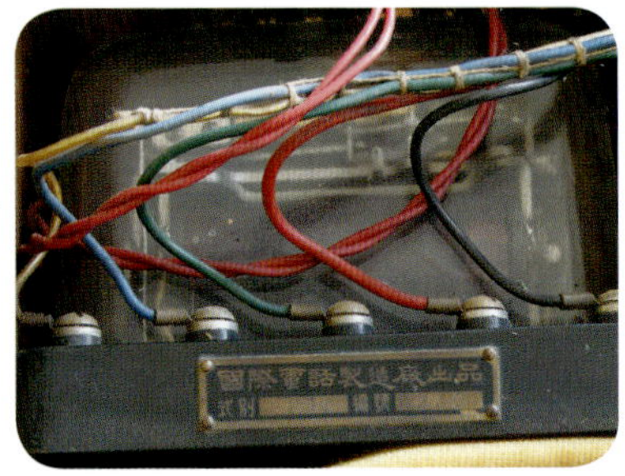

097 电话选别器

年代：1949年

生产：中国国际电话公司

Selector of Dispatching Telephone System

Year: 1949

Producer: International Telephone Company of China

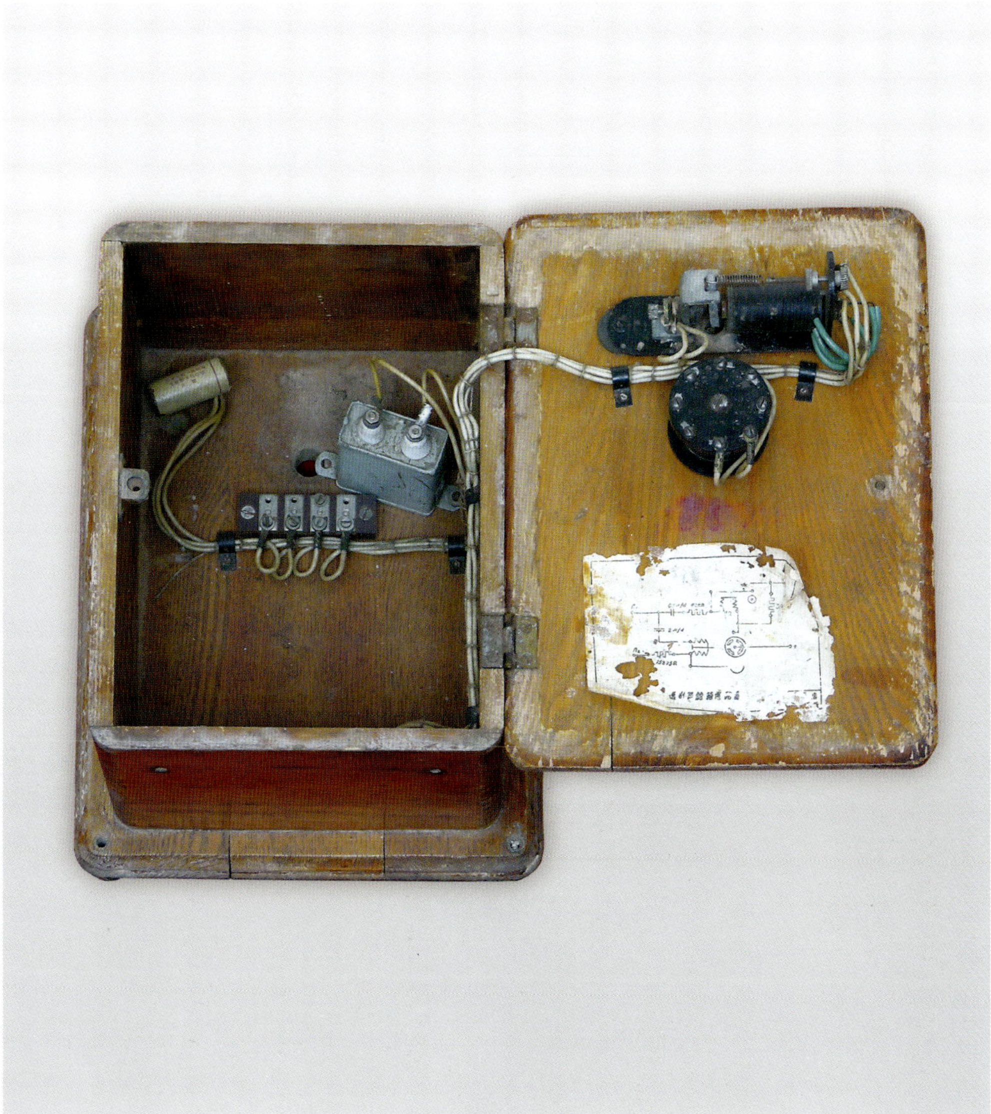

098 电话选别器铃箱

年代：1958年

生产：北京长辛店通讯工厂

Selector of Dispatching Telephone System's Bell Box

Year: 1958　　Producer: Beijing, China

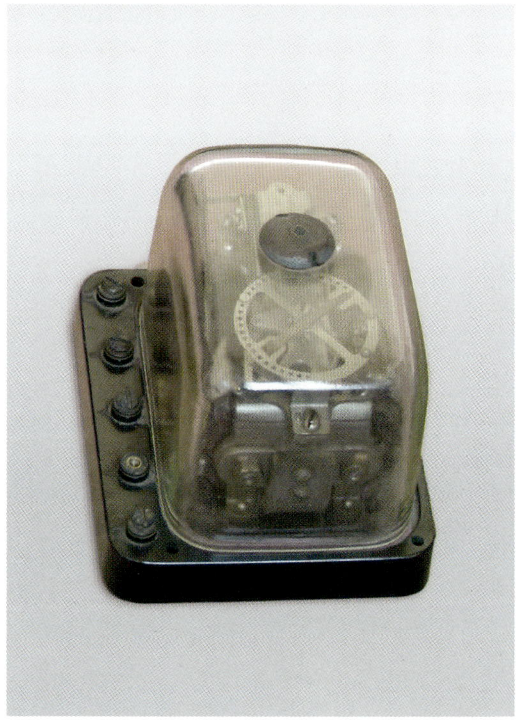

099 调度电话选别器

年代：1950年

Selector of Dispatching Telephone System

Year: 1950

100 客车照明马灯（三级文物）

年代：1910 ~ 1945年

Hurricane Lamp Used in Passenger Car（National Grade-three Cultural Relic）

Year: 1910~1945

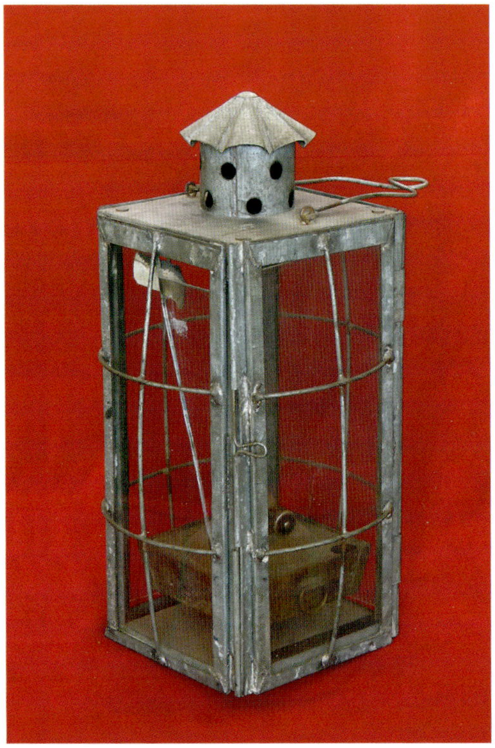

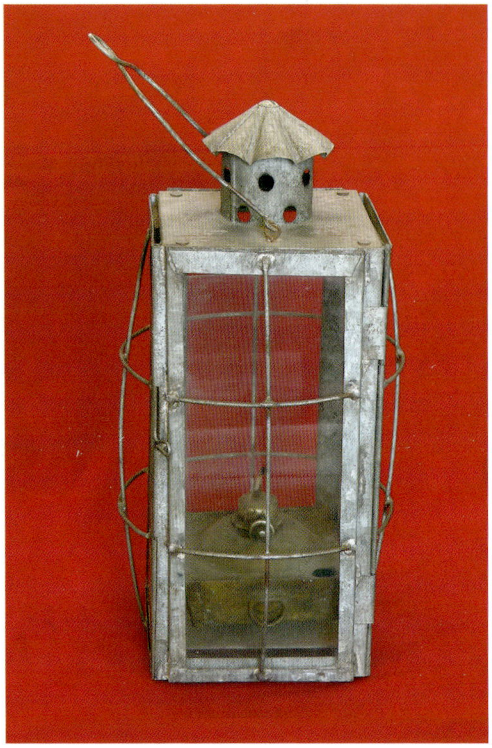

101 客车照明马灯（三级文物）

年代：1910 ~ 1945年

Hurricane Lamp Used in Passenger Car（National Grade-three Cultural Relic）

Year: 1910~1945

102 调车信号灯（三级文物）

年代：1910 ~ 1945年

Shunting Signal （National Grade-three Cultural Relic）

Year: 1910~1945

103 乙炔气体照明灯（三级文物）

年代：1940年

Acetylene Lamp Used in Passenger Car （National Grade-three Cultural Relic）

Year: 1940

104 路签授受机标志灯（三级文物）

指示列车开行或停止的信号灯。

Indicate Lamp Used in the Period Time of Republic of China （National Grade-three Cultural Relic）

Signal lamp for guiding trains to set out or stop.

105 臂板式信号灯（三级文物）

年代：1945年　　产地：中国

Single Lamp of Soviet Union Type（Signal lamp）（National Grade-three Cultural Relic）

Year: 1945　　Place of production: China

106 臂板信号灯（三级文物）

Single Lamp of Soviet Union Type（Signal lamp）（National Grade-three Cultural Relic）

107 防护信号灯（三级文物）

Signal Lamp Used for Safety（National Grade-three Cultural Relic）

108 调车信号灯（三级文物）

Shunting Signal（National Grade-three Cultural Relic）

109 道岔转辙器信号灯（三级文物）

Signal Lamp Used in Switch of Railway (National Grade-three Cultural Relic)

110 蓄电池信号灯（三级文物）

Storage Battery Signal Lamp（National Grade–three Cultural Relic）

111 调车信号灯（三级文物）

Shunting Signal（National Grade–three Cultural Relic）

响墩为内装微型炸药的薄扁圆盒，是一种通过火车轧压发出响声提示列车前方有险情的防护装置。

A Torpedo is a thin round box containing tiny explosive. When run over by trains, it will make a noise to warn the driver to avoid accidents ahead.

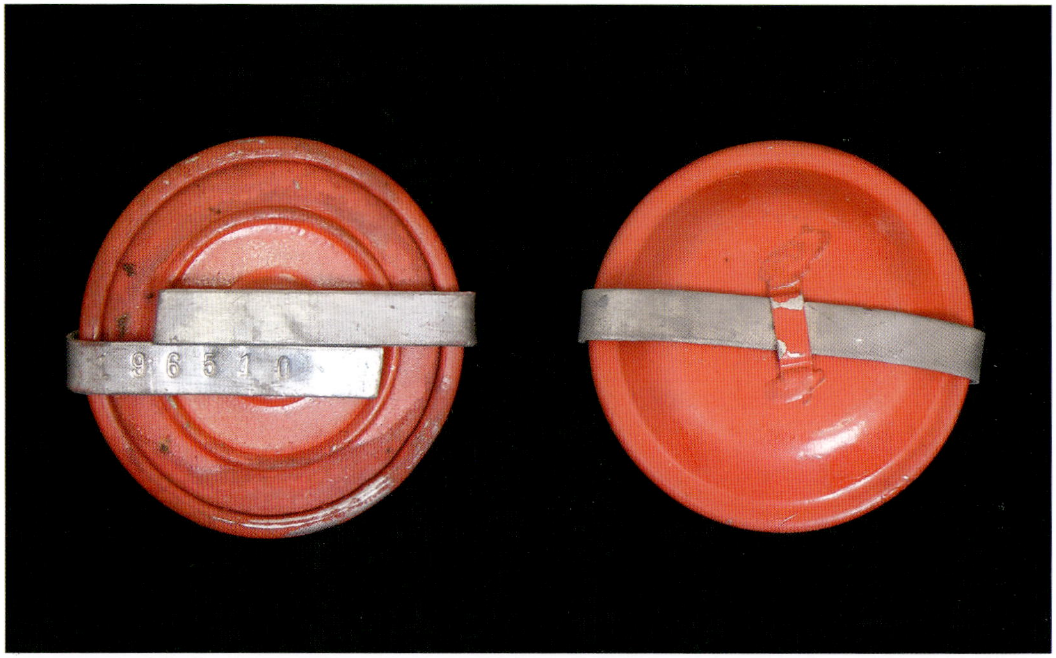

112 红色铁响墩

The Red Iron Torpedo

113 铜响墩

年代：1910年　　产地：法国

Copper Torpedo

Year: 1910　　Place of production: France

114 铜号角

The Cupreous Horn

115 钥匙路签（三级文物）

用途：办理列车通行凭证的设备

年代：1945年　　产地：中国

Train Staff Controlled by Special Keys（National Grade-three Cultural Relic）

Used to check in & out passing trains

Year: 1945　　Place of production: China

4

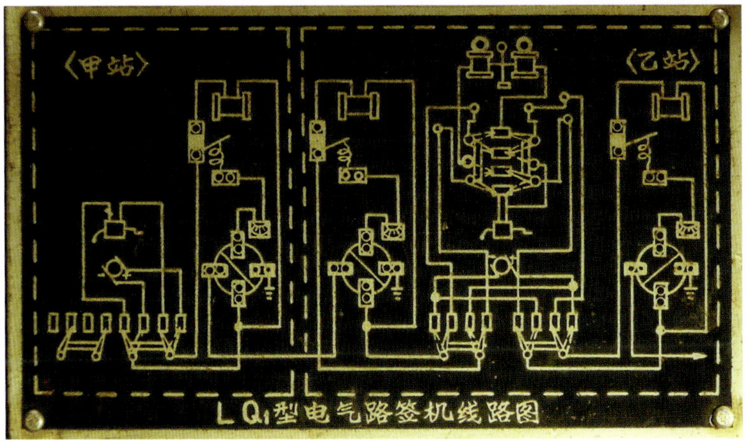

116 苏（联）式电气路签闭塞机（三级文物）

用途：办理列车通行凭证的设备

年代：1950年

Electric Staff-blocking Cabinet（National Grade-three Cultural Relic）

Used to check in & out passing trains

Year: 1950

117 小站半自动闭塞机控制台

用途：小站办理列车通行凭证的设备

Semi-automatic Blocking Controller in Small Stations

Used to check in & out passing trains in small stations

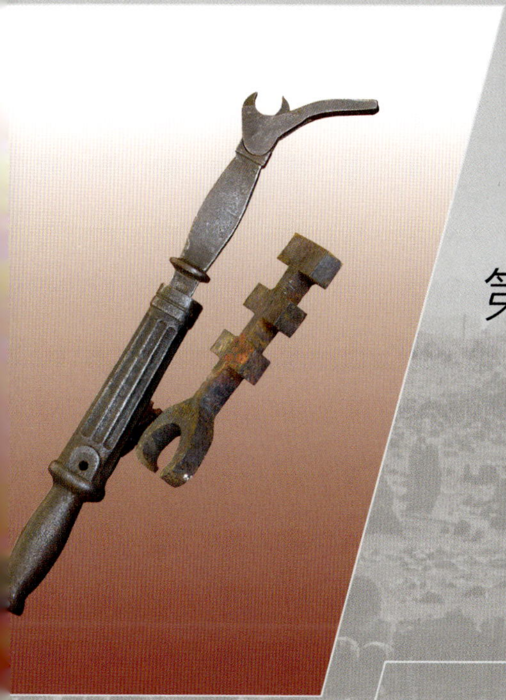

第5章

Article fifth

配件工具

Parts and Tools

开凿坚硬的岩石，挖掘险峻的山洞，架起高耸的桥梁，铺筑钢铁的线路，铁路劳工的每一滴血汗都溶进了铁路的身躯。他们充满粗糙老茧的双手在用过的各种工具和配件上，印刻了铁路劳工坚忍不拔的劳动创造和智慧人生。

Cutting hard rocks, digging steep tunnels, building high-rise bridges and paving railway tracks, workers merged every drop of their blood and sweat into these railways. The persistence of hard work and life of wisdom were marked on various parts and tools in railway workers' calloused hands.

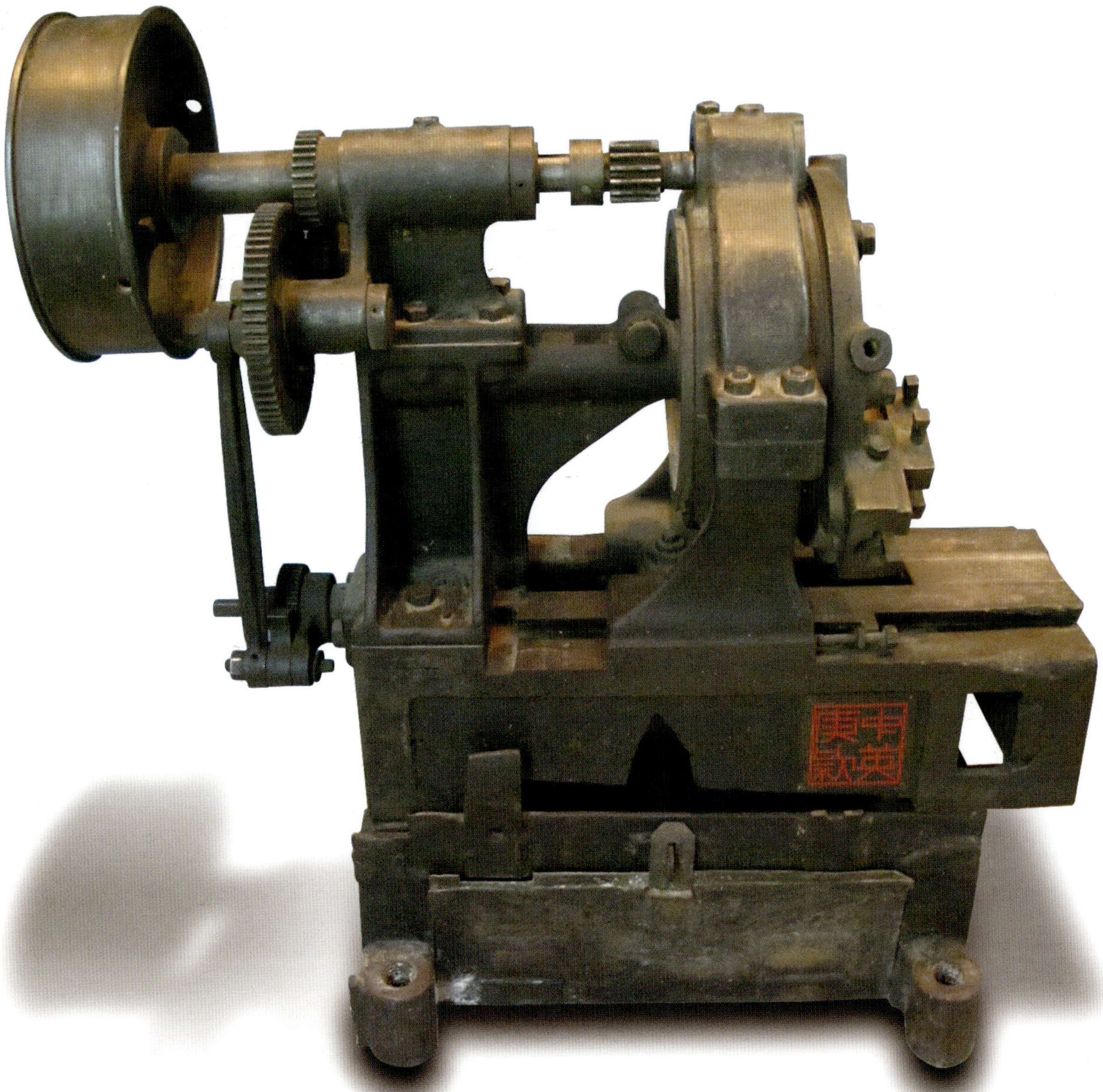

118 机车曲拐销加工机（三级文物）

二战时期，英国用1900年中国清朝赔付的“庚子赔款”购买车床等设备，用于支援中国抗战（史称中英庚款）。

年代：1940年　　产地：英国

Crankpin Processing Machine for Locomotive（National Grade-three Cultural Relic）

During the World War II, Britain purchased machines with the money paid by China of Qing Dynasty to support China's Anti-Japanese War. ("The Boxer Indemnity between China and Britain" in history)

Year: 1940　　Place of production: England

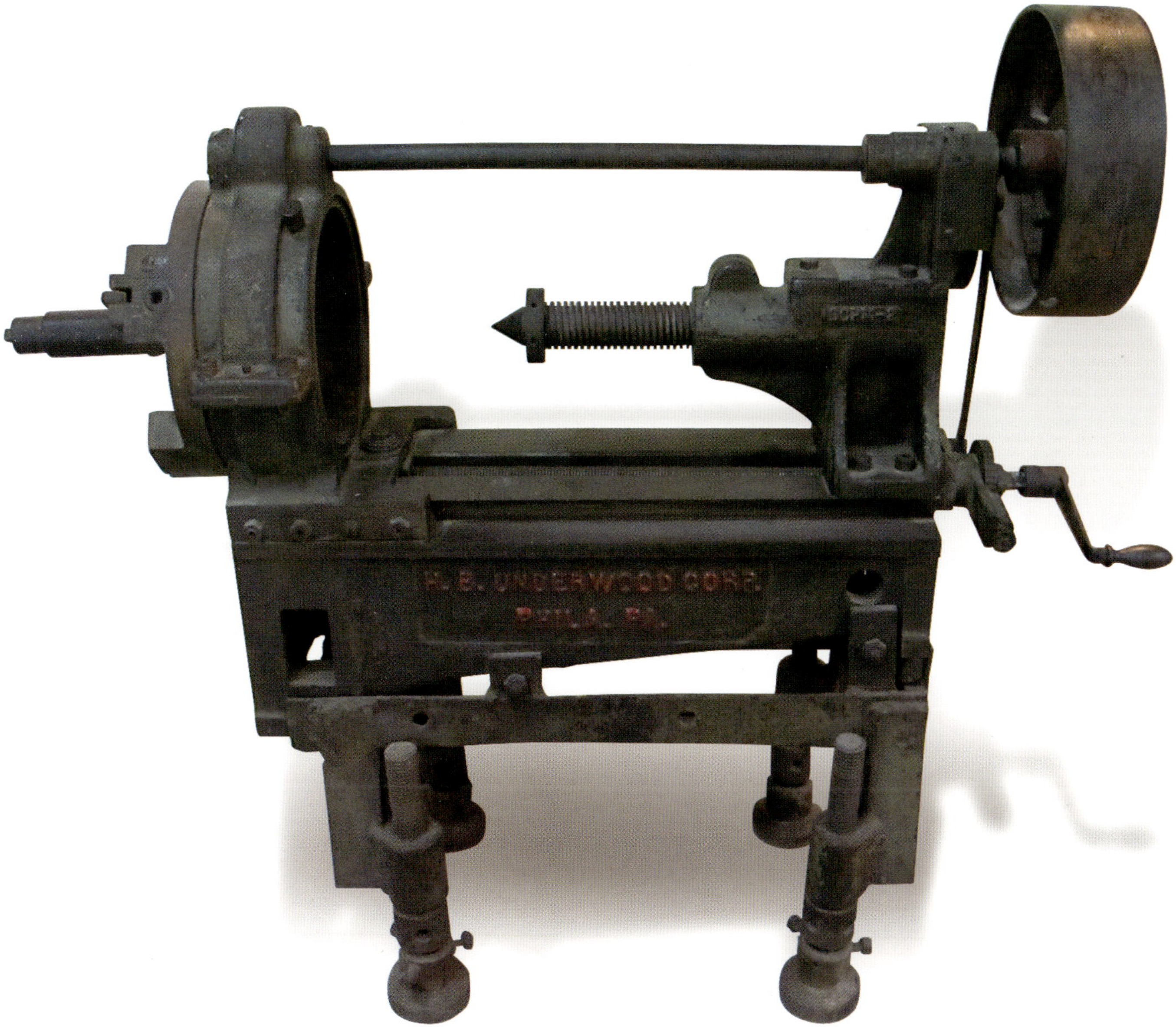

119 机车曲拐销正机（三级文物）

年代：1930~1940年

产地：美国

Crankpin Adjusting Machine for Locomotive （National Grade-three Cultural Relic）

Year: 1930~1940

Place of production: U.S.A

120 镗缸机（三级文物）

产地：美国

Boring and Grinding Machine（National Grade-three Cultural Relic）

Place of production: U.S.A

121 双丝杆走镐（双向螺纹千斤顶）

年代：1930年　　产地：法国

Moveable Ground Jack（Bidirectional Screw Jack）

Year: 1930　　Place of production: France

122 机械顶镐（齿条千斤顶）

年代：1920年　　产地：美国

Rack Pick（Rack Jack）

Year: 1920　　Place of production: U.S.A

123 50吨机械顶镐（齿条千斤顶）

年代：1930 ~ 1940年　　产地：美国

50t−lifting Jack（Rack Jack）

Year: 1930~1940　　Place of production: U.S.A

124 硬木撬棍（二级文物）

年代：1910年　　产地：越南河内

Hard Wooden Crowbar（National Grade-two Cultural Relic）

Year: 1910　　Place of production: Hanoi, Vietnam

125 铁质撬棍

年代：1910年　　产地：法国

Steel Crowbar

Year: 1910　　Place of production: France

126 铁锤

Hammer

127 汲水式消防栓

年代：1928年　　产地：中国

Fire Plug

Year: 1928　　Place of production: China

128 通信电杆避雷针

年代：1910年　　产地：法国

Lightning Rod of the Communication Pole

Year: 1910　　Place of production: France

129 起钉器

年代：1930年　　产地：法国

A Nail Puller

Year: 1930　　Place of production: France

130 钳形万能电表

Universal Clamping Ammeter

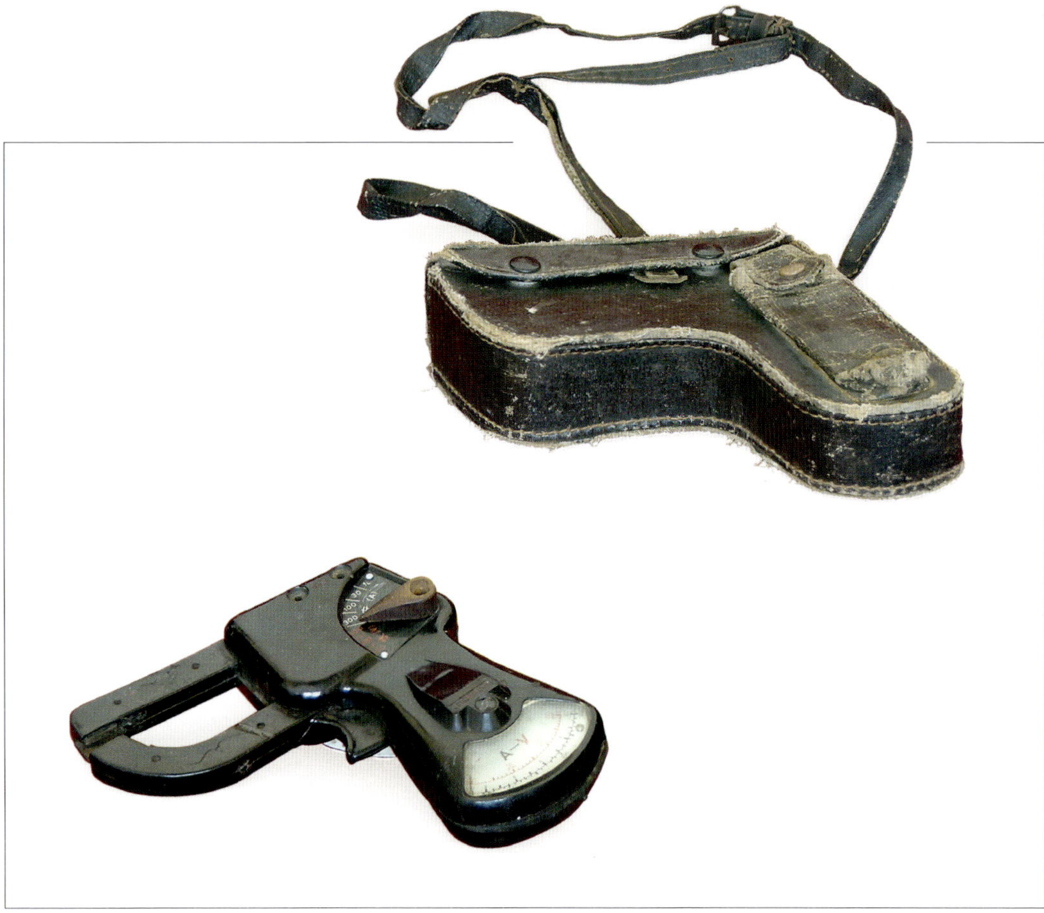

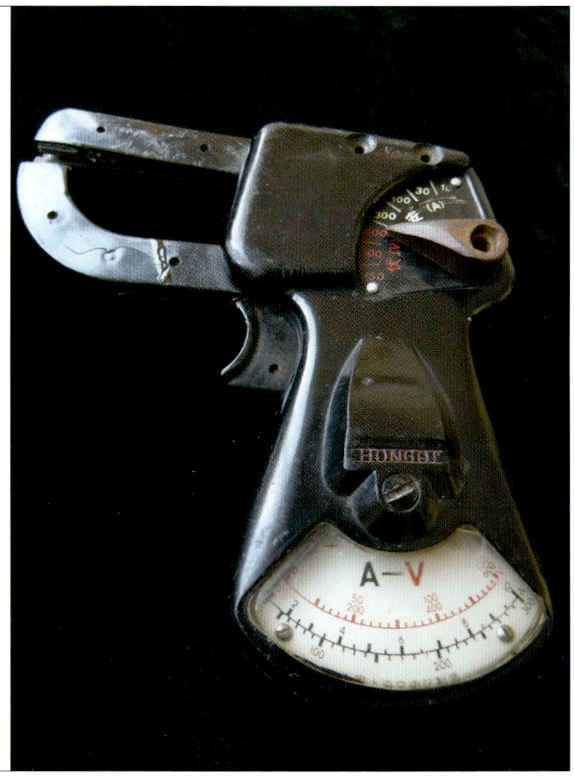

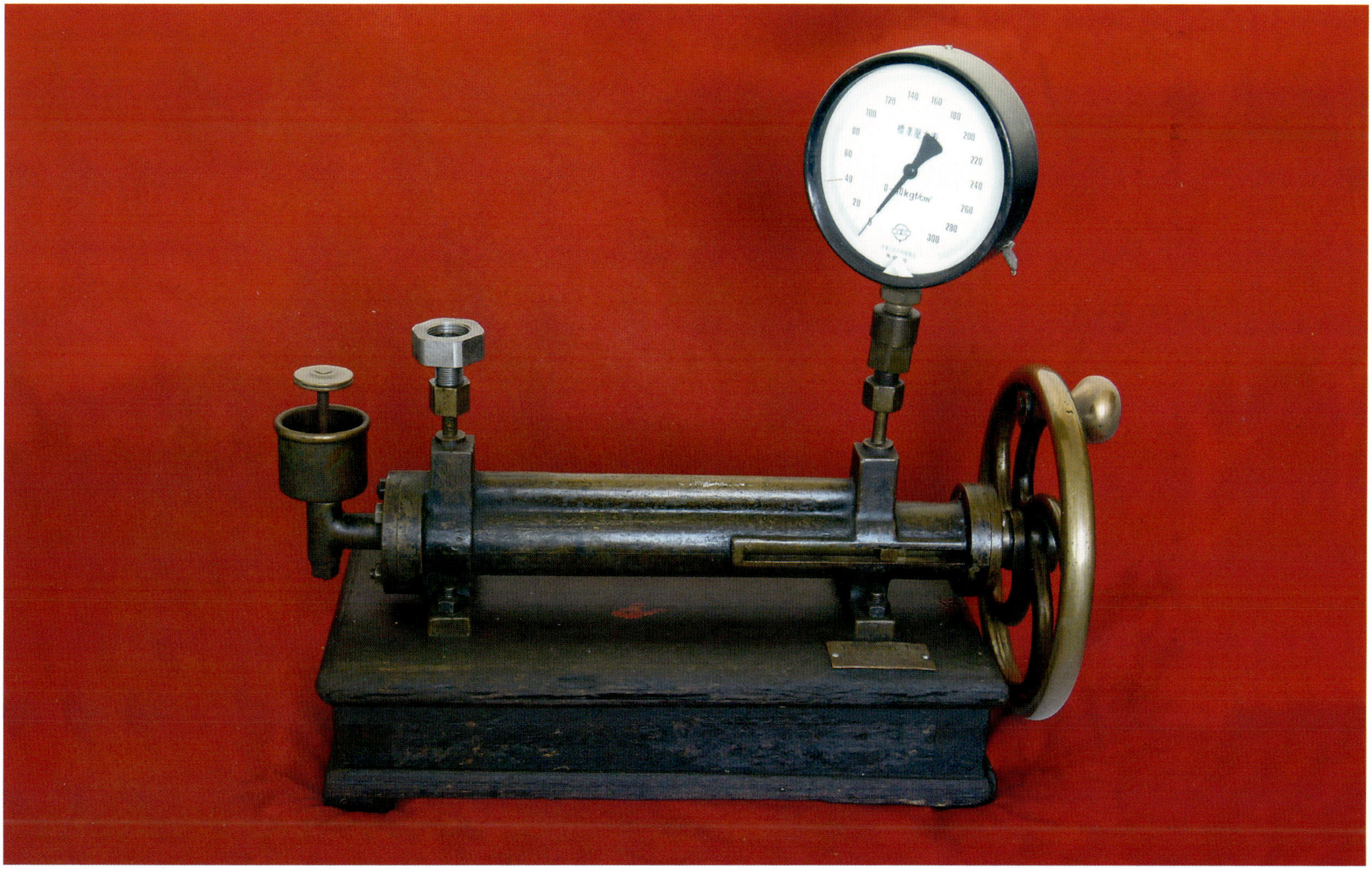

131 压力表检测仪

年代：1940年　　产地：英国

Pressure Instrumentation

Year: 1940　　Place of production: England

132 机车压力表

年代：1850年　　产地：美国

Locomotive Manometer

Year: 1850　　Place of production: U.S.A

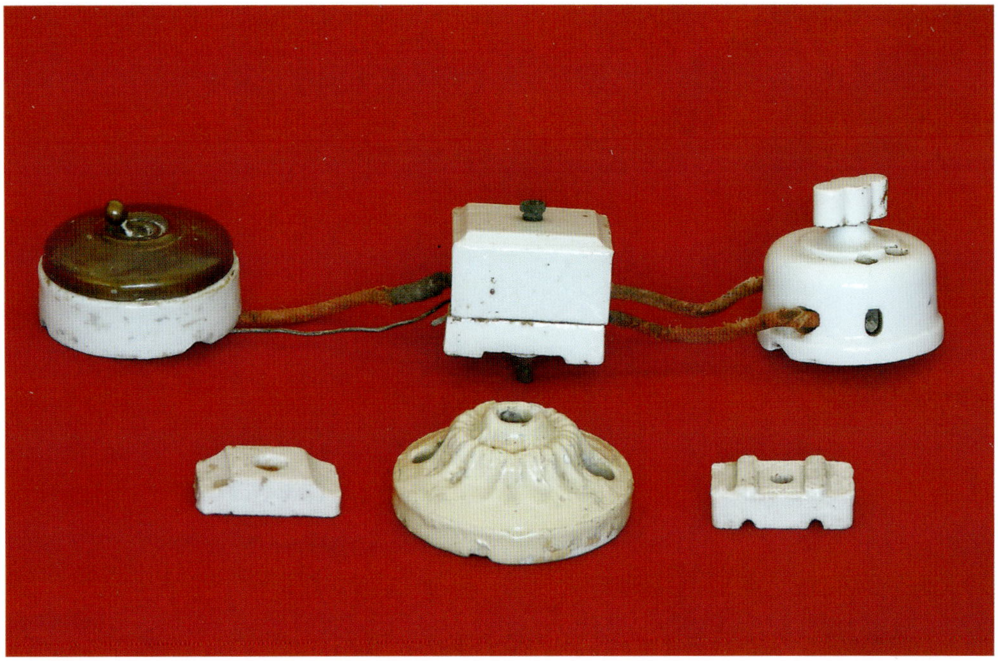

133 电气开关及瓷座、瓷夹

年代：1910年　　产地：法国

Electric Switch and Porcelain Base & Clamps

Year: 1910　　Place of production: France

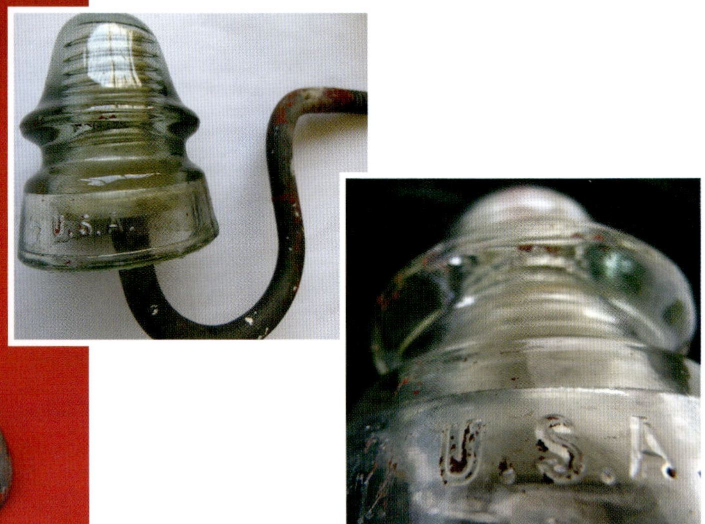

134 玻璃电磁瓶

年代：1920年　　产地：美国

Glass Bottle of Magnetic and Electric

Year: 1920　　Place of production: U.S.A

135 水鹤（三级文物）

水鹤的用途是为过往列车的蒸汽机车加水。材质是铸铁和铸铜。1921年法国制造。个碧石铁路乍甸火车站使用。

Water Crane（National Grade-three Cultural Relic）

Made of casting iron and copper in France in 1921, it was used on Zhadian Railway Station (belonging to Gejiu-Bisezhai-Shiping Railway Company). The function of the water crane is to supply water to passing steam locomotives.

136 蒸汽泵

用途：以蒸汽为动力的水泵，用于车站供水。

年代：1905年　　产地：英国

Steam Pump

Pumps, powered by steam, are used to supply water in stations.

Year: 1905　　Place of production: England

137 手摇齿轮传动轨道车（三级文物）

年代：19世纪　　产地：法国

Hand Operating Mechanical Transmission Railcar （National Grade-three Cultural Relic）

Year: 19th century　　Place of production: France

昆明北
CÔN-MINH BẮC
联运
LIÊN VẬN

第6章 Article sixth

铭牌标志

Nameplates and Signs

人有名字，物有名称。每一枚铭牌都是表明自己身份信息的标志。在铁路机车、车辆、桥梁、钢轨、机床、时钟、甚至砖瓦、保险柜等设备之上，大都标注它们不同的归属和时代。列车方向牌则是告诉旅客乘车方向和车次的引导指示牌。还有铁路员工佩带的工种号牌等，表明的是铁路这部大联动机协调运转的分工与合作。在博物馆中展示的这些铭牌和标志，深深地留下了云南铁路不可磨灭的历史烙印和文化标识。

As everything in the world has a name, each nameplate is used to identify equipment that wears it. Different origins and completion dates are labeled on most equipments such as locomotives, vehicles, bridges, rails, machine tools, clocks and even bricks,safes. Direction signs show passengers direction and number of the train. What is more, coordination and distribution of responsibilities are demonstrated on different signs worn by different workers. In a word, the history and culture of Yunnan railway deeply left marks on these nameplates and signs shown in our museum.

138 臂章

Armband

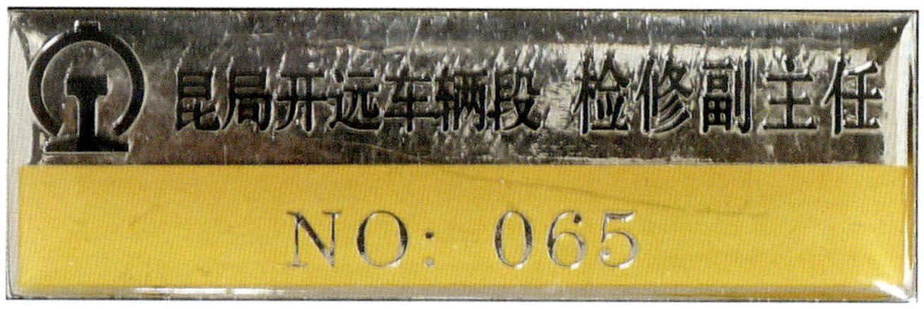

139 胸牌

Chest Card

140 L.DENIS公司桥梁铭牌（三级文物）

Bridge Nameplate Made by L.DENIS Company（National Grade-three Cultural Relic）

141 蒸汽机车铭牌（三级文物）

The Nameplate of JF_{51} Locomotive（National Grade-three Cultural Relic）

142 模范机车荣誉匾

1958年原铁道部将山西、郑州等铁路局部分机车改造后，分批调入云南铁路使用，此荣誉匾为机车上铭牌。

Honor Plaque for Model Locomotive

In 1958, the Railways Administration at that time transferred parts of improved locomotives to Yunnan railways from several railway administrations of Shanxi, Zhengzhou etc. This Honor plaque is hung on one of those locomotives.

143 波贝梅·马尔邦铸造厂车辆铭牌（三级文物）

The Nameplate of the Car Made in Baume et Marpent（National Grade-three Cultural Relic）

年代：1905年　　Year: 1905

144 圣·德尼公司车辆铭牌（三级文物）

Bridge Nameplate by St.Denny Company（National Grade-three Cultural Relic）

年代：1903年　　Year: 1903

145 法·比公司车辆铭牌（三级文物）

The Nameplate of the Car by France-Belgium Company（National Grade-three Cultural Relic）

年代：1902年　　Year: 1902

146 法·比公司车辆铭牌（三级文物）

The Nameplate of the Car Made in France-Belgium Company（National Grade-three Cultural Relic）

年代：1923年　　Year: 1923

147 日本川崎造船所KD_{55}米轨蒸汽机车铭牌（三级文物）

The Nameplate of KD_{55} Locomotive Made in Japan（National Grade-three Cultural Relic）

148 东风号蒸汽机车铭牌（三级文物）

The Nameplate of "Dongfenghao" Locomotive（National Grade-three Cultural Relic）

1958年，昆明机车修理厂仿造法式MK_{51}型四台机车，并对原设计做了若干改进。由当时中共云南省委副书记马继孔命名为“东风号”。

Kunming Locomotive Repair Plant made four locomotives by imitating French MK_{51} and did some improvements in 1958. This model of cars was named "Dongfenghao" by Ma Jikong, the deputy secretary of Yunnan provincial party committee then.

149 合众机械公司车床铭牌

年代：20世纪30年代　　产地：美国

A Nameplate of A Turning Machine Made by Allied Machinery Company（National Grade-three Cultural Relic）

Year: 1930s　　Place of production: U.S.A

150 劳动工具厂车库公英制换算表（三级文物）

年代：20世纪20年代　　产地：美国

A Copper Table for Converting Metric and British System Made by the American Tool Works. Co.（National Grade−three Cultural Relic）

Year: 1920s　　Place of production: U.S.A

151 滇越铁路公司2752号保险柜铭牌（三级文物）

年代：20世纪20年代　　产地：法国

No.2752 Nameplate of A Safe（National Grade−three Cultural Relic）

Year: 1920s　　Place of production: France

152 沙厘爺银行保险柜铭牌（三级文物）

The Nameplate for the Safe used by Charrier & Cie Fichet Foreign Firm（National Grade −three Cultural Relic）

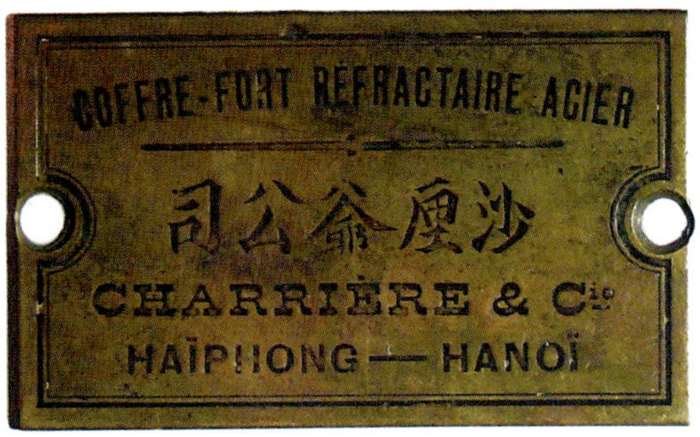

153 “个碧临屏铁路公司”大门石刻（三级文物）

该石刻位于原个碧石铁路公司大门门头，历史上曾被拆除，后经多方寻找收藏，仅“公”字遗失。

年代：1926年

The Stone Carving at the Gate of Gejiu-Bisezhai-Shiping Railway Company（National Grade-three Cultural Relic）

This stone carving was at the gate of Ge-bi-shi Railway Company but removed in the history. After searching from multiple aspects, it has been almost intact except for the loss of "公".

Year: 1926

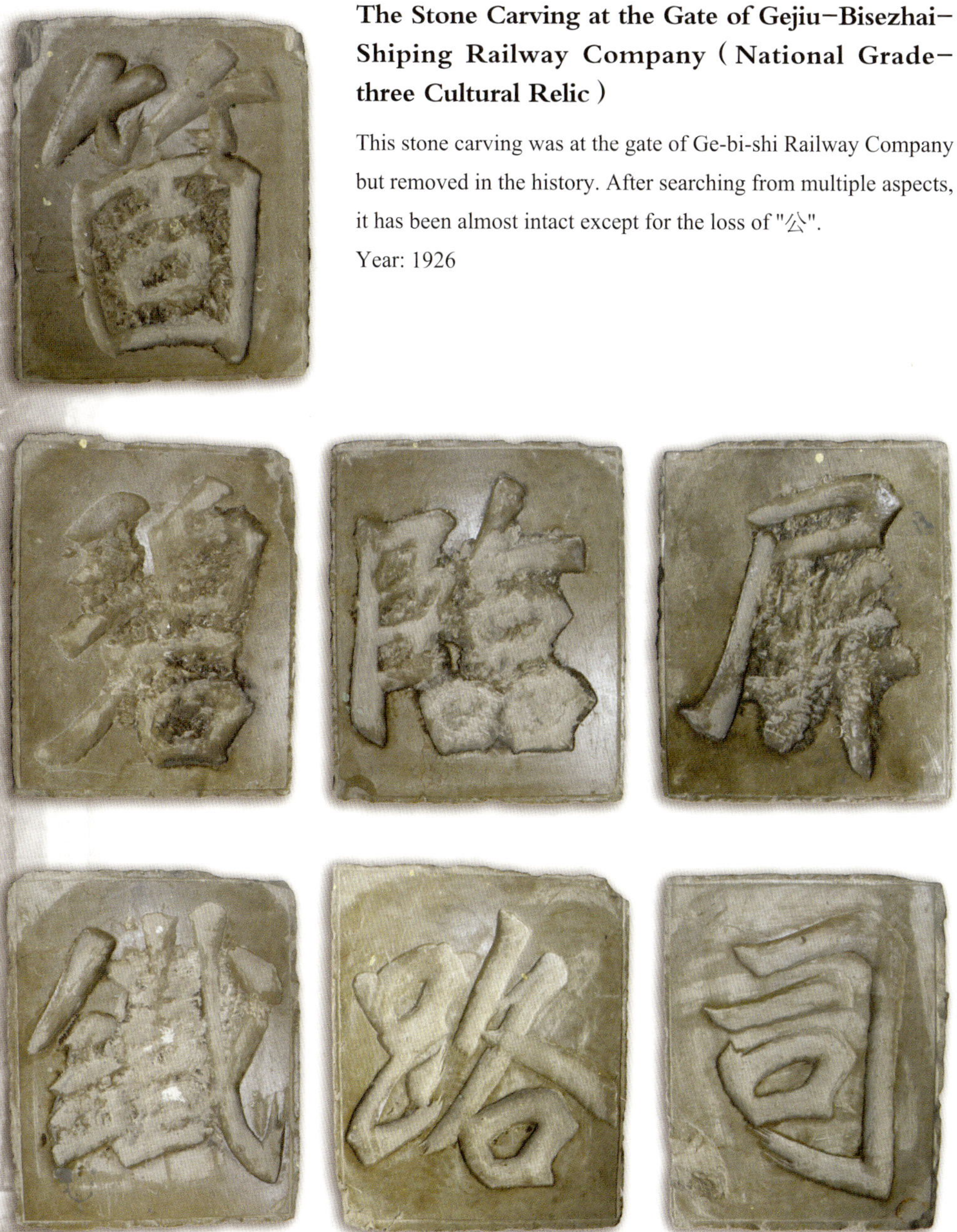

154 **米轨中越国际联运列车方向牌**

The Direction Board of China-Vietnam International Through Transport for 1000mm Gauge

155 列车方向牌

云南铁路曾经使用过的列车方向牌。左页为中国昆明至越南河内国际联运列车上的方向牌。

The Direction Board

Direction Boards used by Yunnan railways. On Left page is the direction board on Kunming of China-Vietnam International through Transport.

准轨

米轨

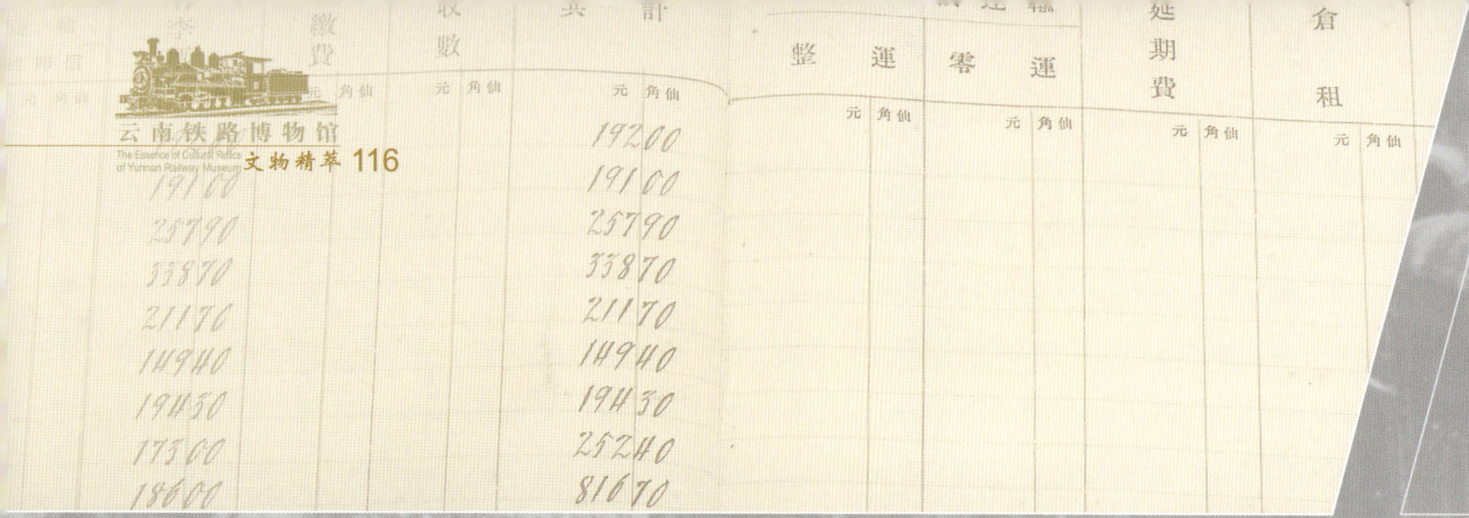

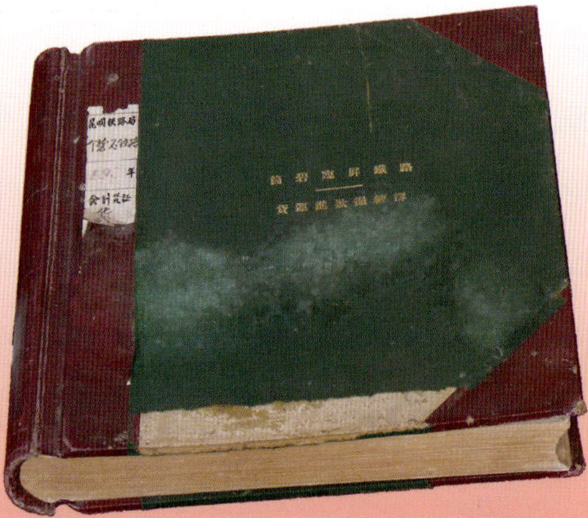

PETITE VITESSE
de HAIPHONG
à MONGTZEU PICHETCHAI

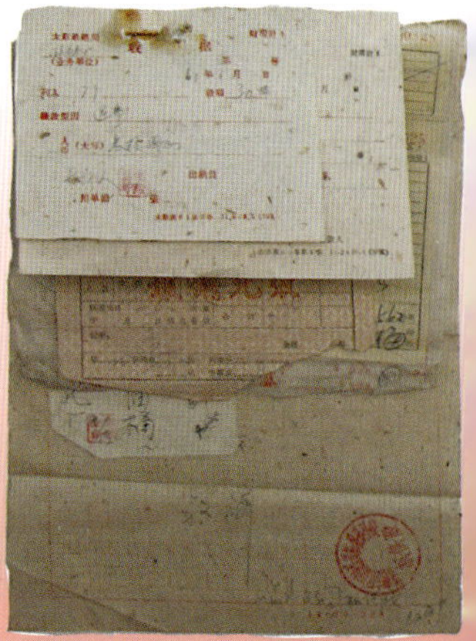

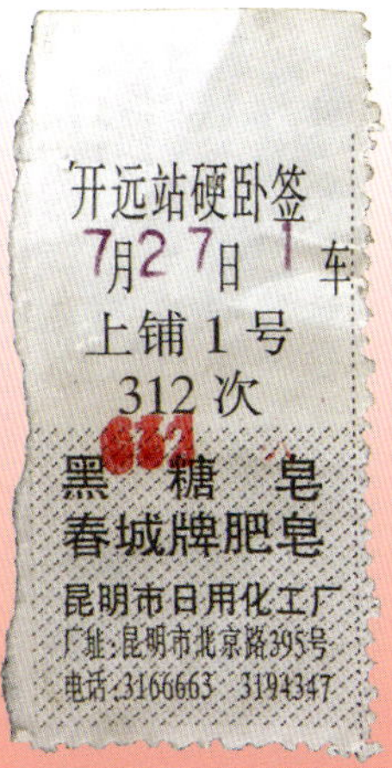

第7章

Article seventh

票证票据

Tickets and Bills

旅客车票、货物运单、车厢号牌等等，也许简单地只是一个凭证，但我们同样可从中发现蕴含在字里行间的历史启迪，因为它们是铁路运输生产中旅客流动、货物周转和职工人事变动的证明，是一个时代工农业、商贸业发展乃至一个国家和地区经济社会状态的写照。

Things like passenger tickets, cargo waybills, and carriage numbers are more than certificates, but valuable historic legacies. Not only are they the proof of passenger flow, cargo turnover and personnel change, but also the reflection of agricultural, industrial and commercial development, and even of economic and social status in this country and region at that time.

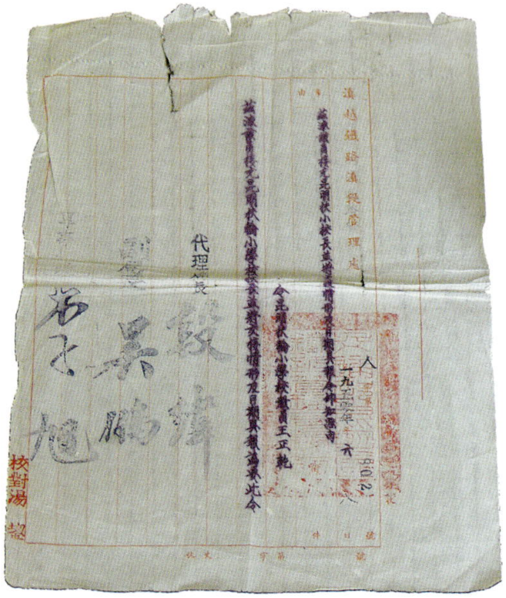

156 滇越铁路管理局人事令［人字第802号］

Personnel Transfer Order Issued by Yunnan-Vietnam Railway Administration [Personnel No.802]

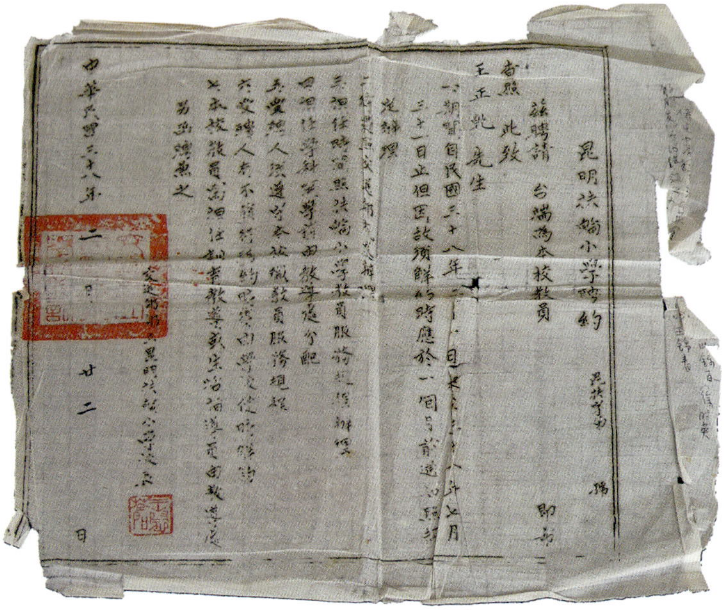

157 昆明扶轮小学聘约

昆明扶轮小学为铁路早期的职工子弟学校。

Teacher's Contract of Kunming Fulun Primary School

Kunming Fulun Primary School was a school for children of railway staffs at that time.

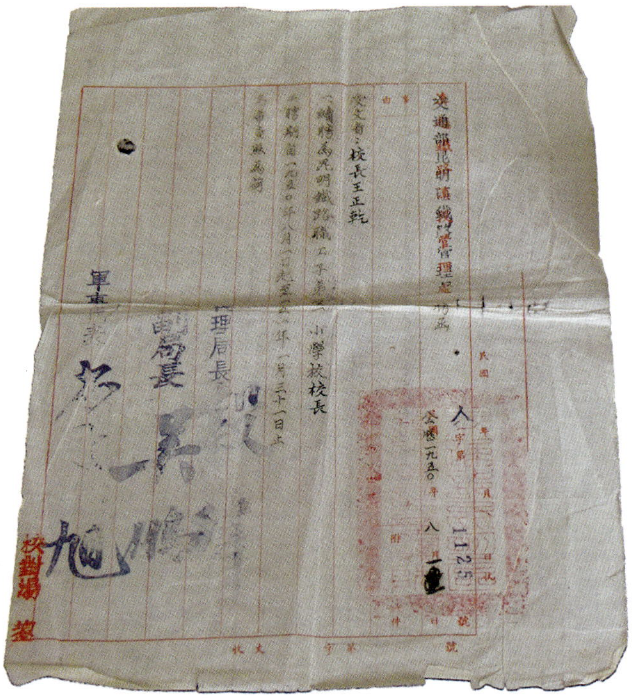

158 交通部昆明滇越铁路管理局转函

Documents of Yunnan-Vietnam Railway Administration

159 滇越铁路职工家属身份证（三级文物）

Staff Dependents ID of Yunnan–Vietnam Railway（National Grade–three Cultural Relic）

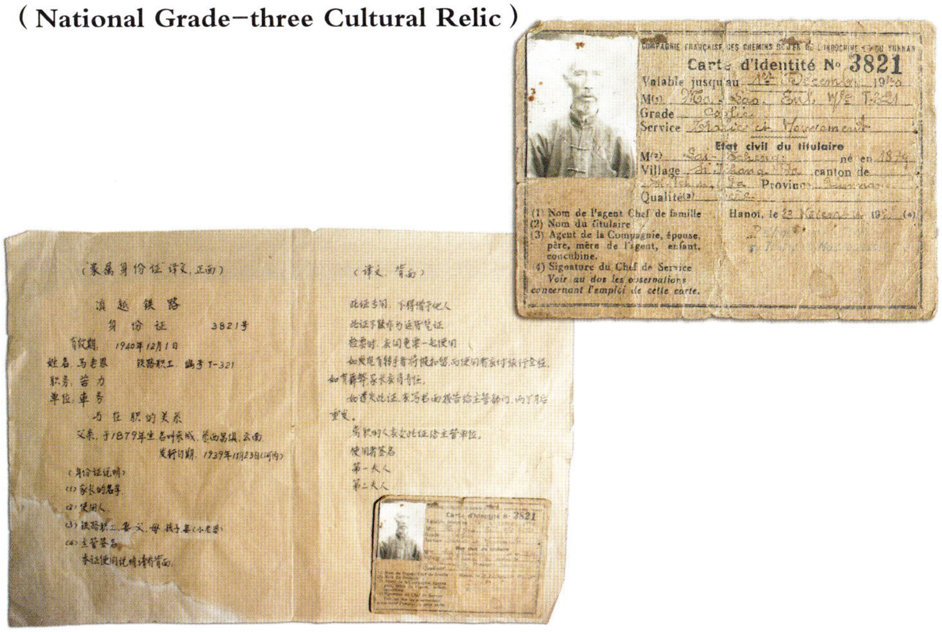

160 昆明铁路区响应云南起义通电（三级文物）

1949年12月9日云南和平起义，昆明区铁路管理局局长唐宇纵电令全局各站段、队、厂、库、全体职工响应起义保护路产。

The telegram of Kunming Railways Administration responding to the Yunnan Uprising（National Grade–three Cultural Relic）

On December 9th, 1949, the Yunnan Uprising began. Tang Yuzong, then-head of Kunming Railways Administration commanded every level of management of his charge and all staffs to respond the Uprising and protect railways.

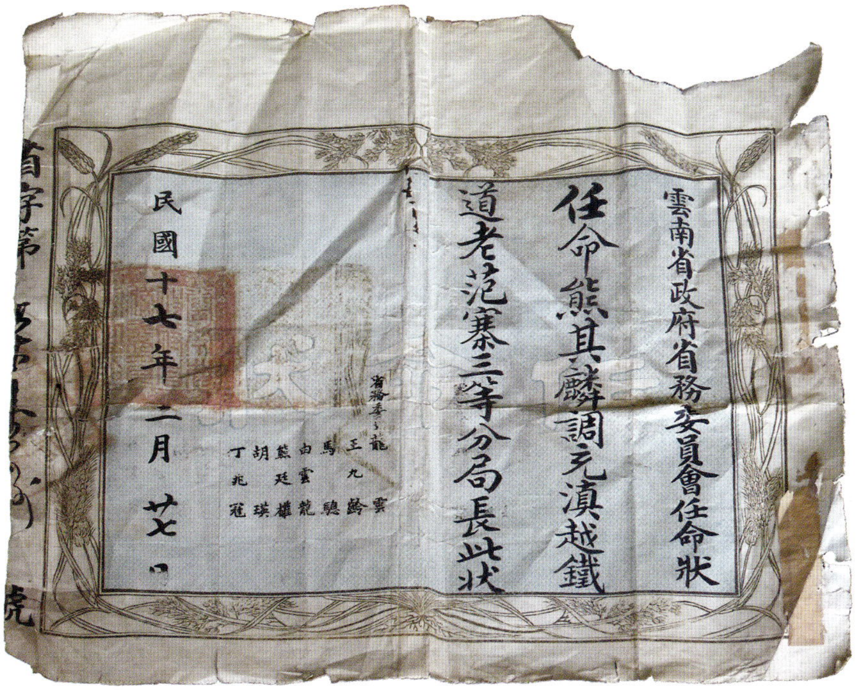

161 民国云南省政府任命状

1928年（民国17年）云南省政府委任驻滇越铁路老范寨警察机构负责人任命状。

Letter of Commission Issued by the Republic Government of Yunnan Province

This is a letter of commission issued by the Republic Government of Yunnan Province to appoint personnel to Laofanzhai Police Station of Yunnan-Vietnam Railway in 1928.

162 滇越铁路法营时期员工履历表

Employment Sheet of Staff of Yunnan-Vietnam Railway

163 滇越铁路公司法籍翻译弗朗索瓦·拜迪

French Interpreter Mr. Francois Petit of Yunnan-Vietnam Railway Company

164 滇越铁路公司中国向导蒋成文

Chinese Guide Mr. Jiang Chengwen of Yunnan-Vietnam Railway Company

165 乘车证

Boarding Card

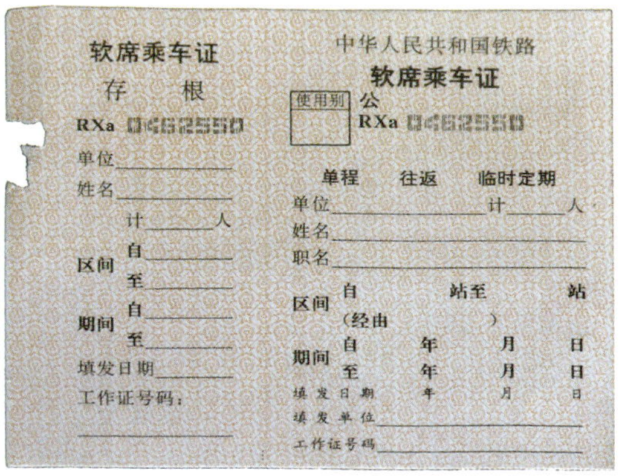
软席乘车证
存 根
RXa 0462550
单位
姓名
计 人
区间 自 至
期间 自 至
填发日期
工作证号码：

中华人民共和国铁路
软席乘车证
使用别 公
RXa 0462550
单程 往返 临时定期
单位 计 人
姓名
职名
区间 自 站至 站
（经由 ）
期间 自 年 月 日
至 年 月 日
填发日期 年 月 日
填发单位
工作证号码

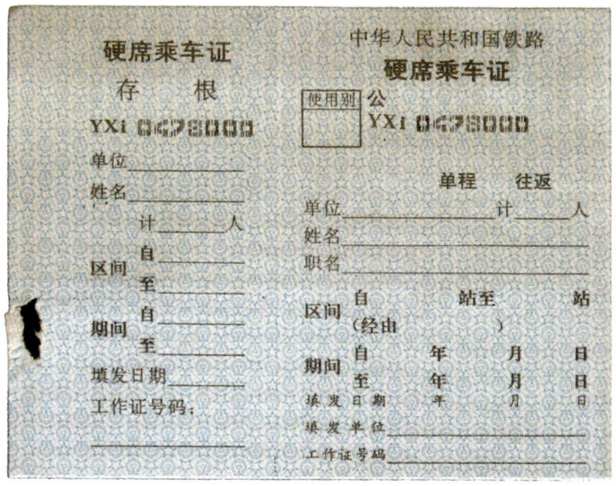
硬席乘车证
存 根
YXl 0478000
单位
姓名
计 人
区间 自 至
期间 自 至
填发日期
工作证号码：

中华人民共和国铁路
硬席乘车证
使用别 公
YXl 0478000
单程 往返
单位 计 人
姓名
职名
区间 自 站至 站
（经由 ）
期间 自 年 月 日
至 年 月 日
填发日期 年 月 日
填发单位
工作证号码

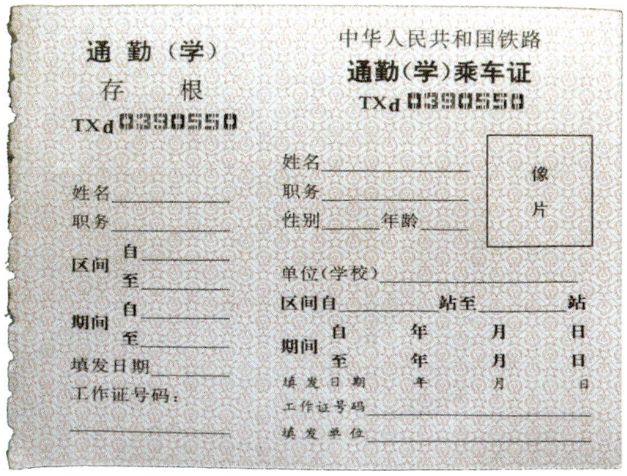
通勤（学）
存 根
TXd 0390550
姓名
职务
区间 自 至
期间 自 至
填发日期
工作证号码：

中华人民共和国铁路
通勤（学）乘车证
TXd 0390550
姓名
职务
性别 年龄
像片
单位（学校）
区间自 站至 站
期间 自 年 月 日
至 年 月 日
填发日期 年 月 日
工作证号码
填发单位

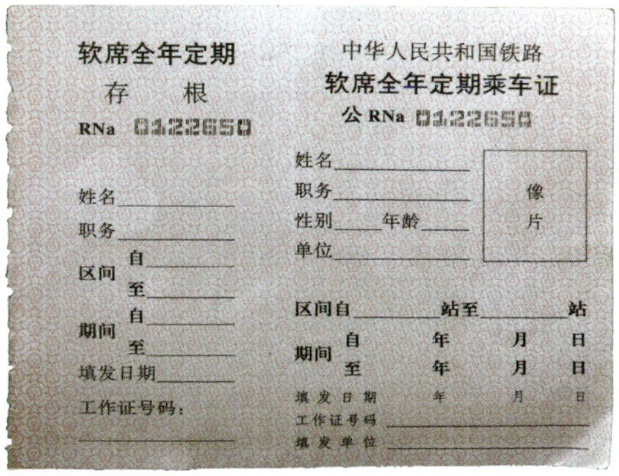
软席全年定期
存 根
RNa 0122650
姓名
职务
区间 自 至
期间 自 至
填发日期
工作证号码：

中华人民共和国铁路
软席全年定期乘车证
公 RNa 0122650
姓名
职务
性别 年龄
单位
像片
区间自 站至 站
期间 自 年 月 日
至 年 月 日
填发日期 年 月 日
工作证号码
填发单位

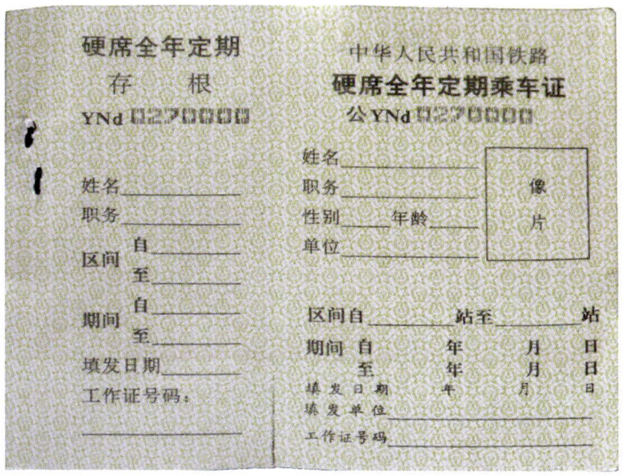
硬席全年定期
存 根
YNd 0270000
姓名
职务
区间 自 至
期间 自 至
填发日期
工作证号码：

中华人民共和国铁路
硬席全年定期乘车证
公 YNd 0270000
姓名
职务
性别 年龄
单位
像片
区间自 站至 站
期间 自 年 月 日
至 年 月 日
填发日期 年 月 日
填发单位
工作证号码

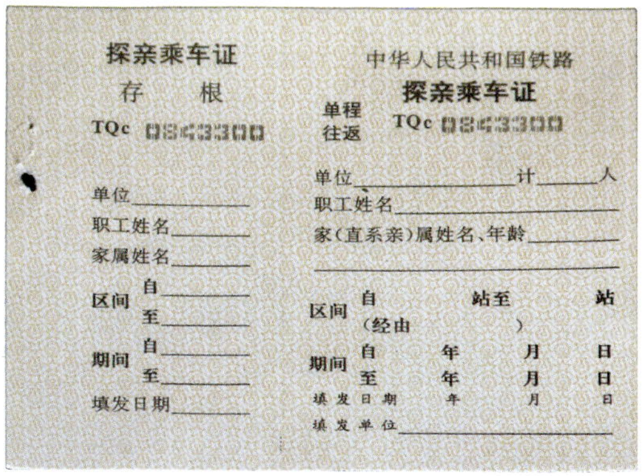
探亲乘车证
存 根
TQc 0843300
单位
职工姓名
家属姓名
区间 自 至
期间 自 至
填发日期

中华人民共和国铁路
探亲乘车证
单程 往返
TQc 0843300
单位 计 人
职工姓名
家（直系亲）属姓名、年龄
区间 自 站至 站
（经由 ）
期间 自 年 月 日
至 年 月 日
填发日期 年 月 日
填发单位

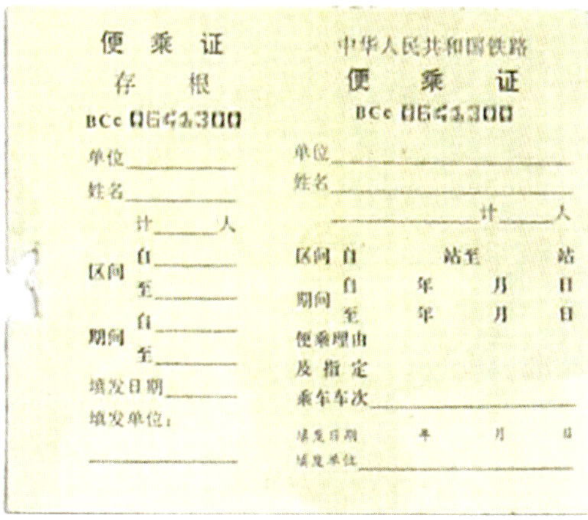
便 乘 证
存 根
BCc 0641300
单位
姓名
计 人
区间 自 至
期间 自 至
填发日期
填发单位：

中华人民共和国铁路
便 乘 证
BCc 0641300
单位
姓名
计 人
区间 自 站至 站
期间 自 年 月 日
至 年 月 日
便乘理由
及指定
乘车车次
填发日期 年 月 日
填发单位

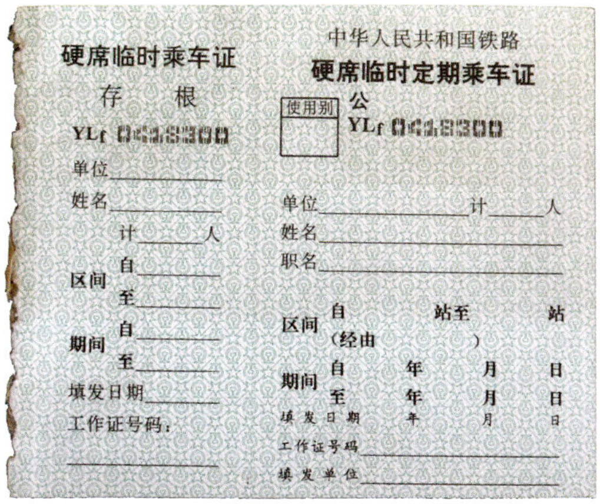
硬席临时乘车证
存 根
YLf 0418300
单位
姓名
计 人
区间 自 至
期间 自 至
填发日期
工作证号码：

中华人民共和国铁路
硬席临时定期乘车证
使用别 公
YLf 0418300
单位 计 人
姓名
职名
区间 自 站至 站
（经由 ）
期间 自 年 月 日
至 年 月 日
填发日期 年 月 日
工作证号码
填发单位

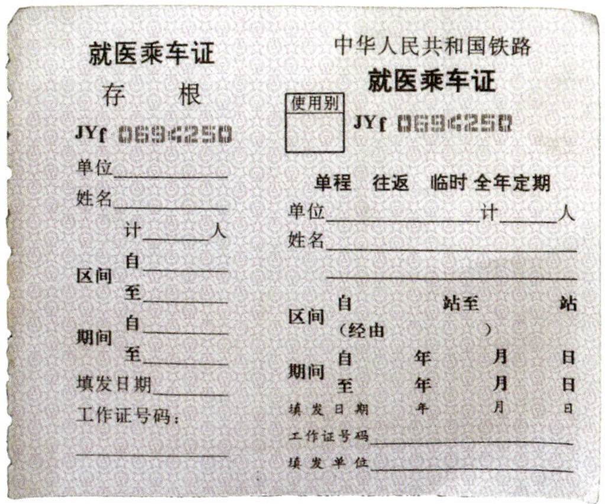
就医乘车证
存 根
JYf 0694250
单位
姓名
计 人
区间 自 至
期间 自 至
填发日期
工作证号码：

中华人民共和国铁路
就医乘车证
使用别
JYf 0694250
单程 往返 临时 全年定期
单位 计 人
姓名
区间 自 站至 站
（经由 ）
期间 自 年 月 日
至 年 月 日
填发日期 年 月 日
工作证号码
填发单位

166 解款清单

List of Transferring Funds

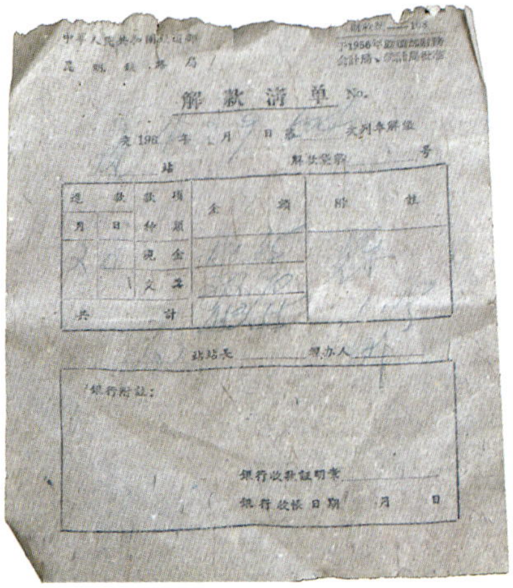

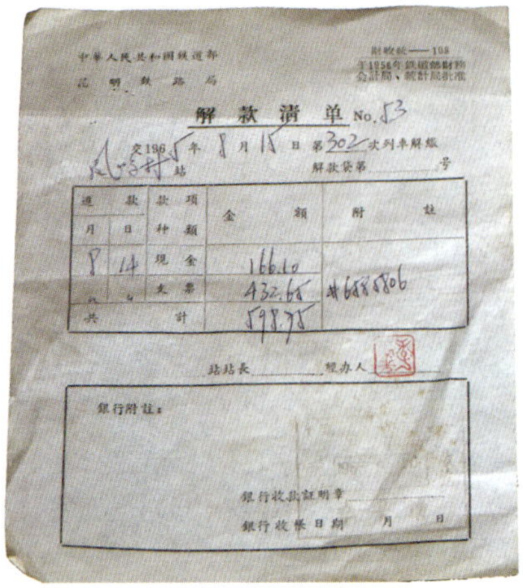

167 货物运送单

List of Cargo Tranfer

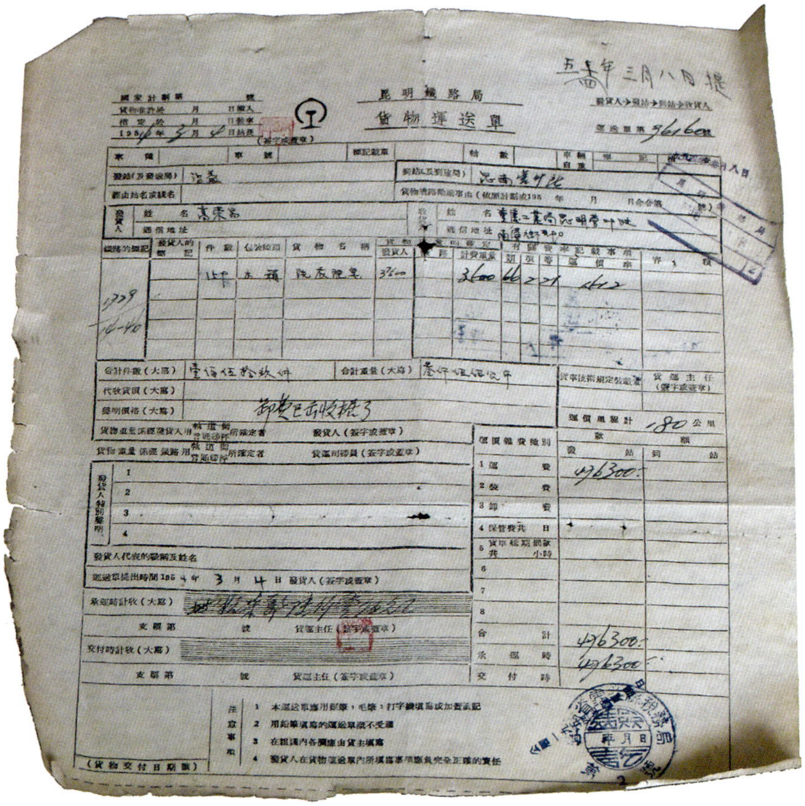

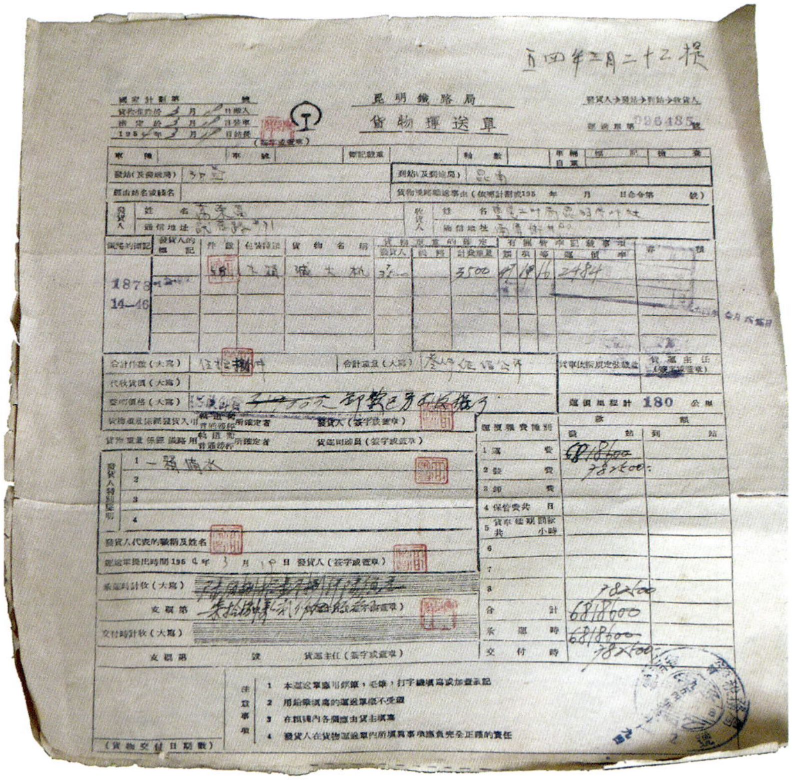

168 《个碧石铁路货运进款册》

The Volume of Freight Income from Gejiu-Bisezhai-Shiping Railway

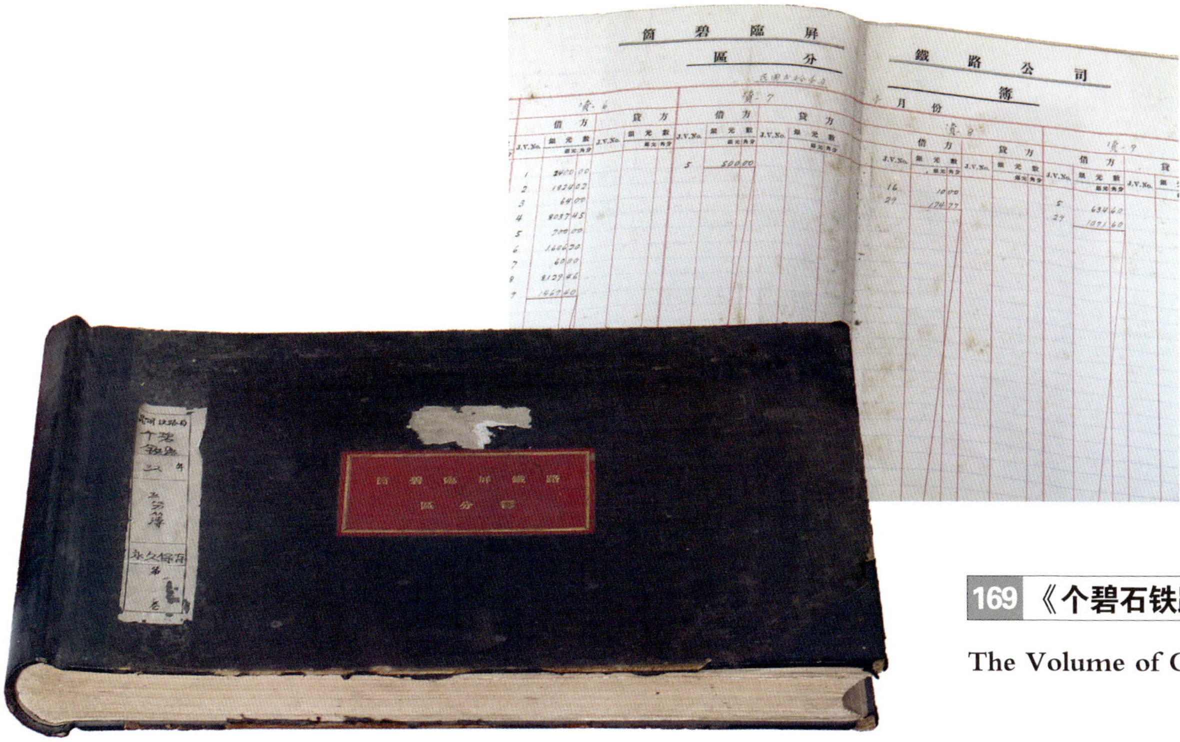

169 《个碧石铁路临屏区分簿》

The Volume of Gejiu-Bisezhai-Shiping Railway

170 客票和货票

Passenger Tickets and Cargo Tickets

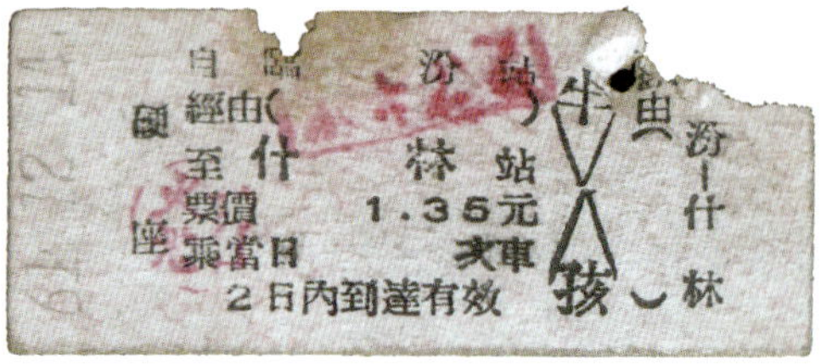

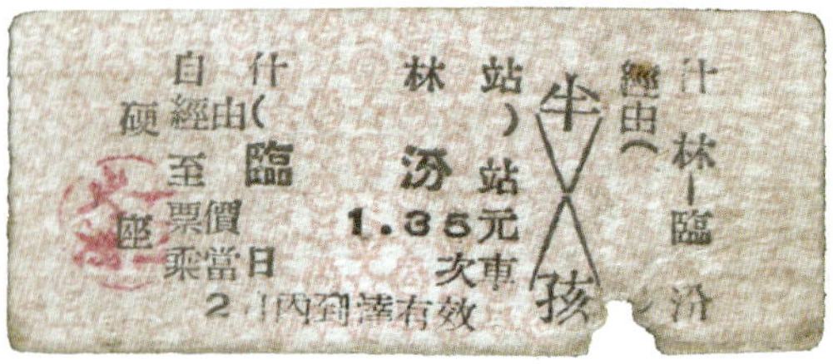

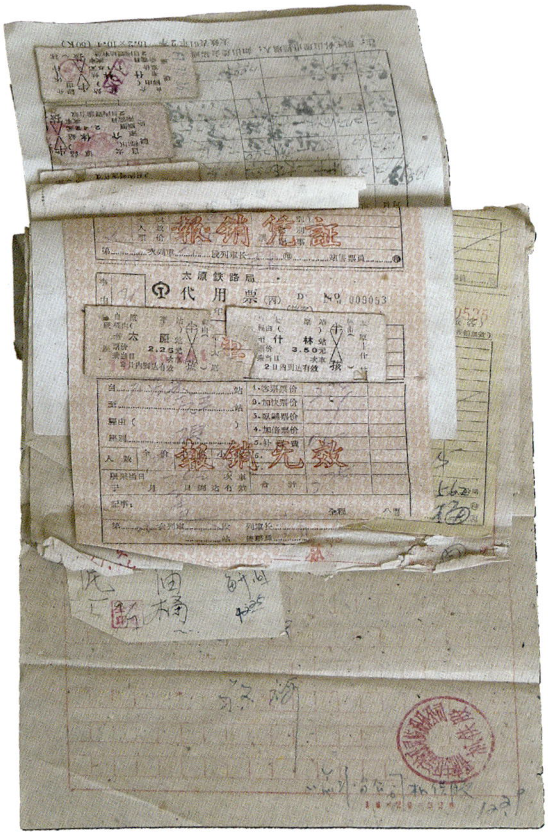

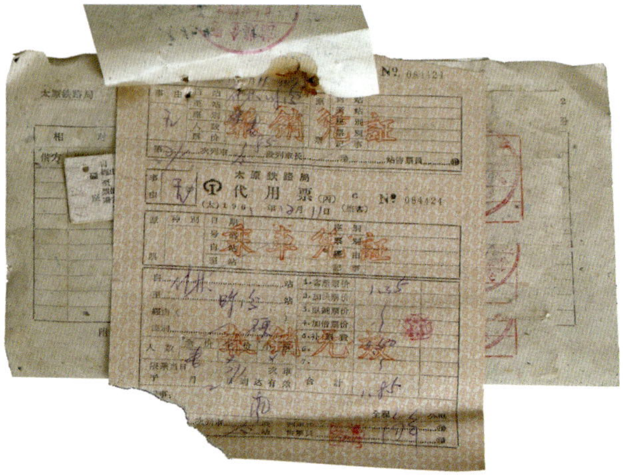

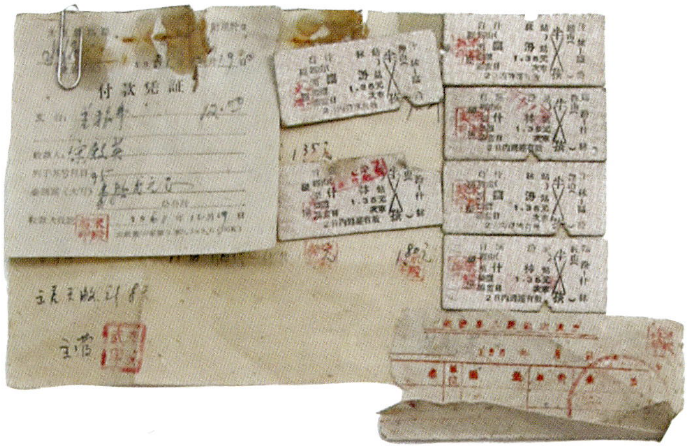

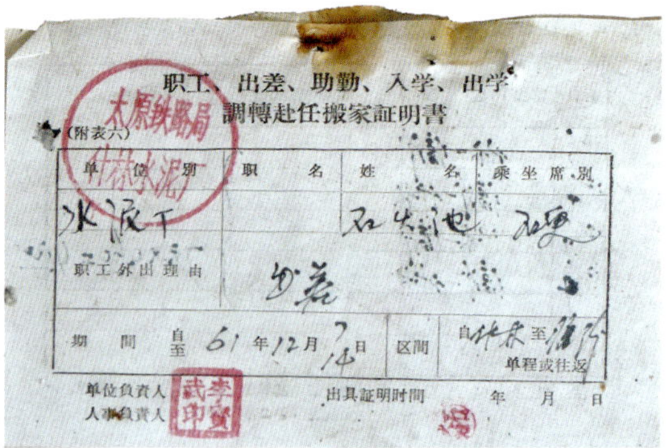

171 换票皮夹和换票证

Check-in Notecase and Check-in Invoice

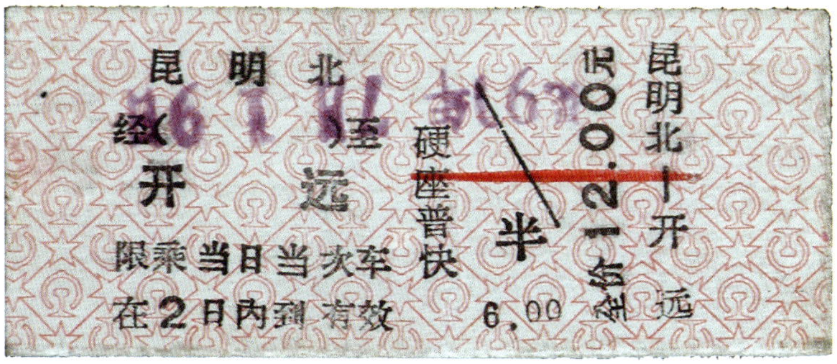

172 昆明北—开远火车票

Tickets of Train from Kunming North to Kaiyuan

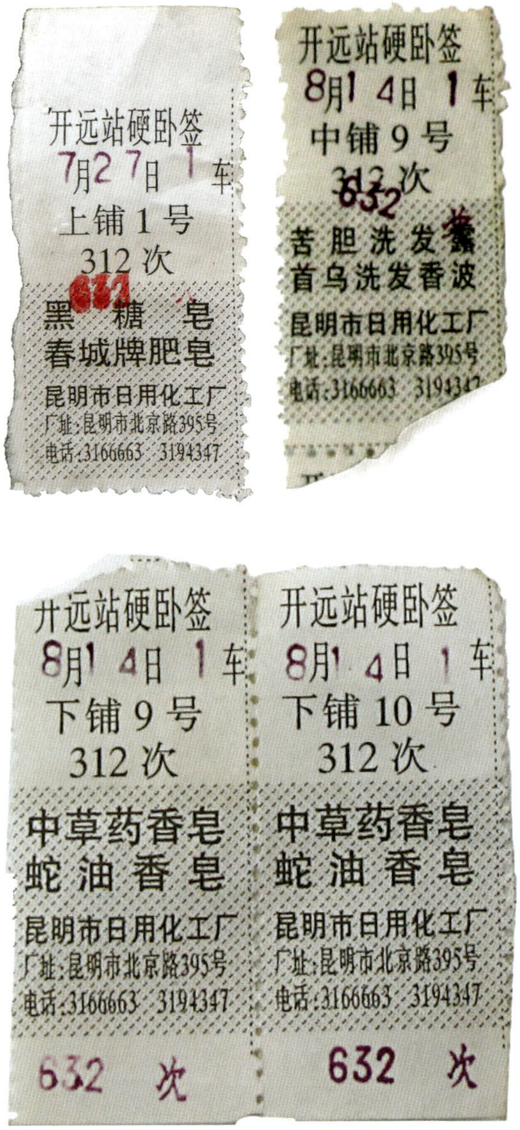

173 开远站硬卧签

Hard-Seat Tickets of Kaiyuan Railway Station

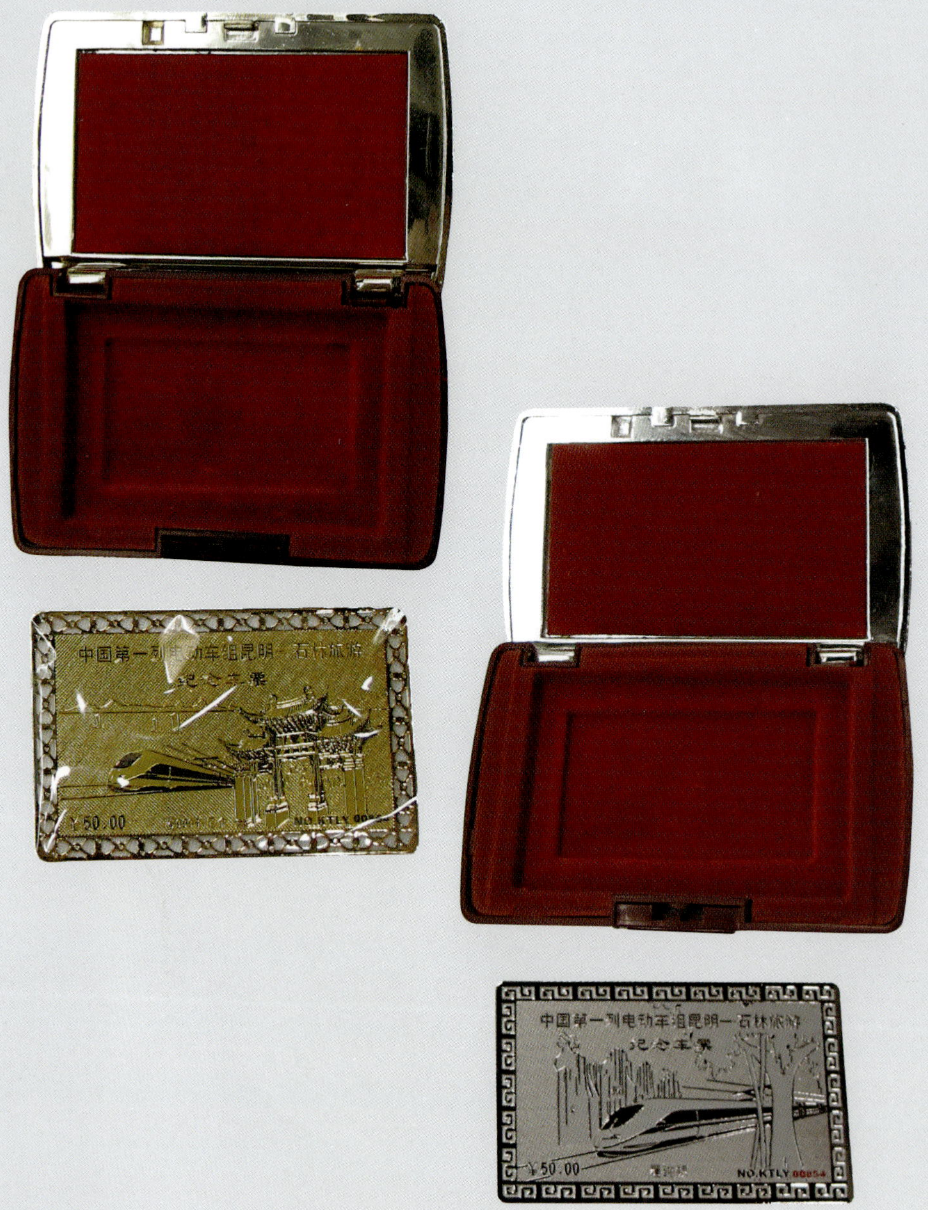

174 昆明—石林旅游纪念车票

Souvenir Travel Ticket from Kunming to Shilin

175 解款袋

Security Bags for Transferring Funds

176 司机手帐

火车司机工作的记录簿。

Driver's Notepad

A notepad for train drivers to document their work

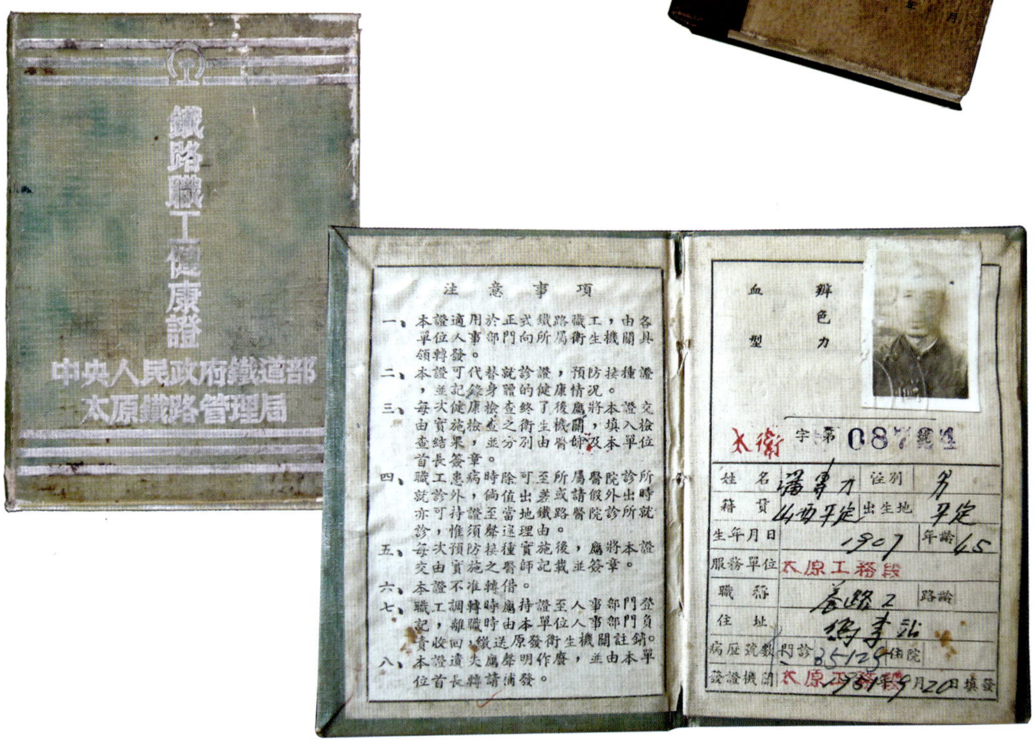

177 铁路职工健康证

Health Certificate of Railway Staffs

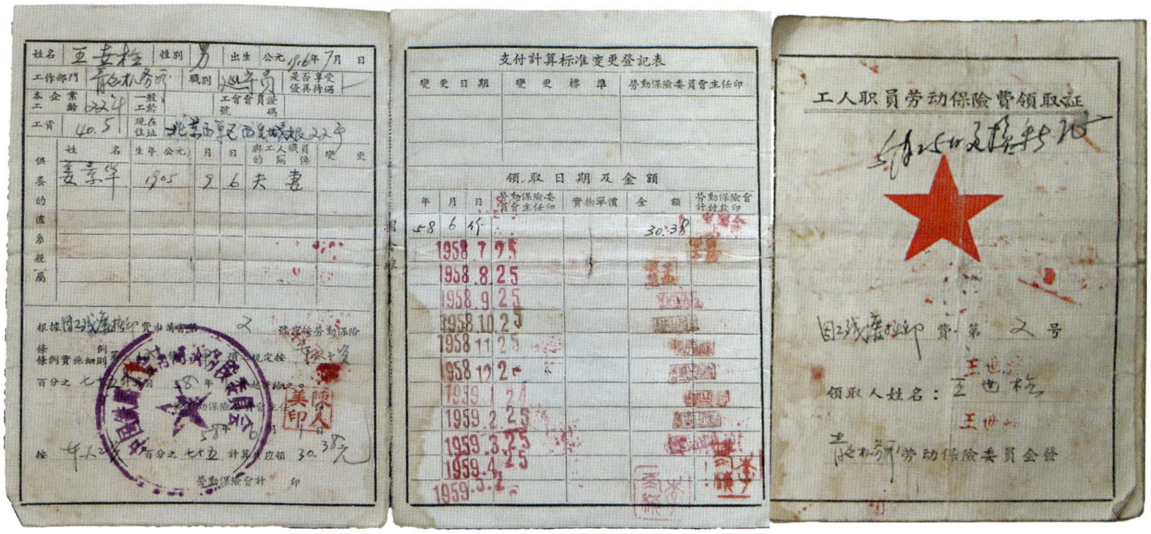

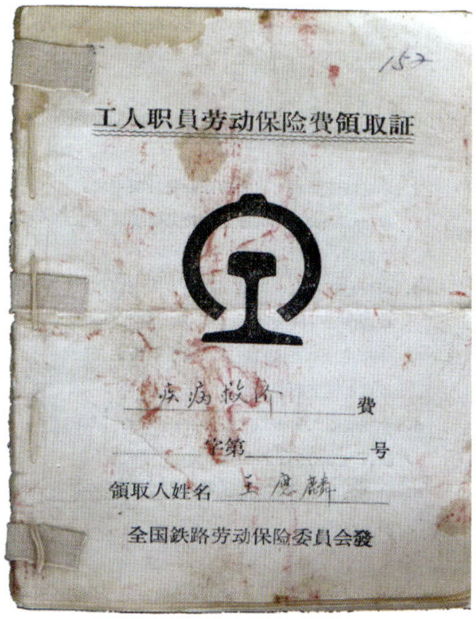

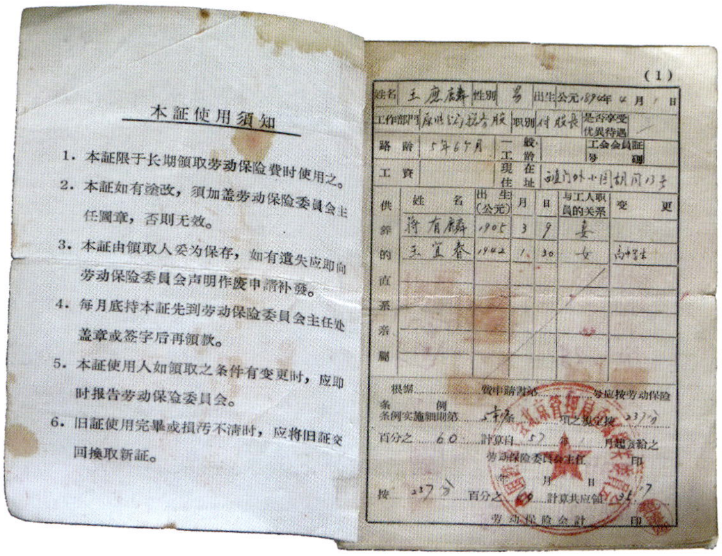

178 工人职员劳动保险费领取证

Labor Insurance Card of Staffs

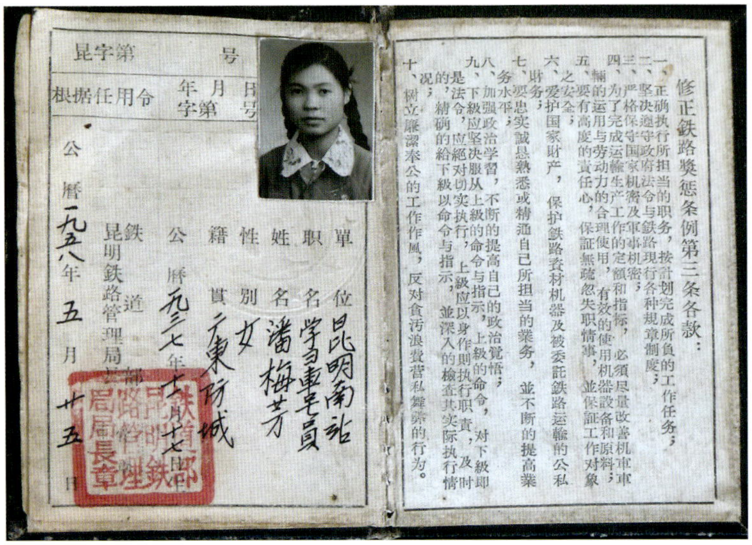

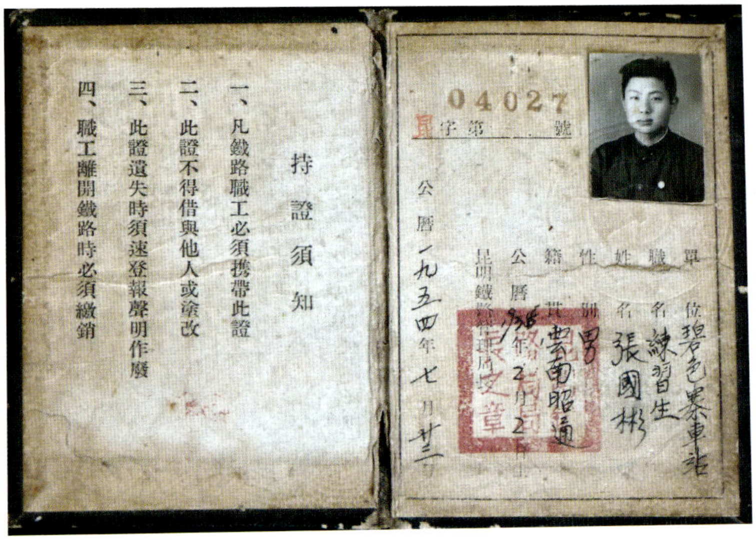

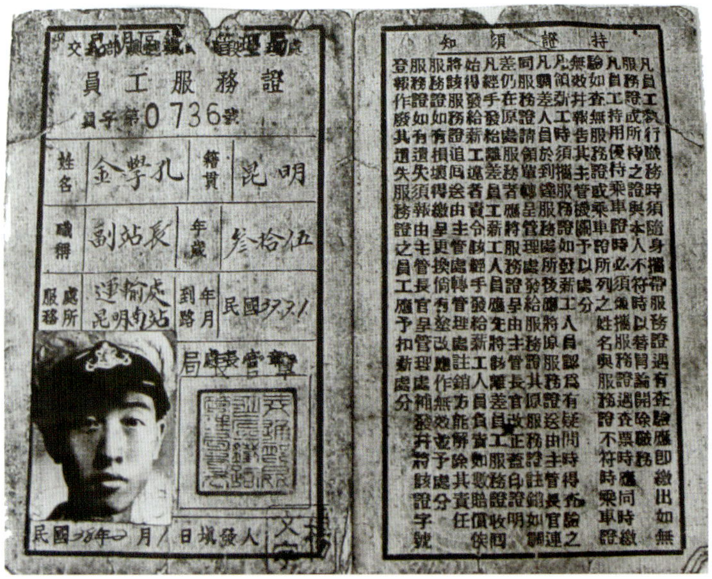

179 铁路员工服务证

Service Card of Staffs

180 铁路员工服务证[第0736号]

Service Card of Staffs [No. 0736]

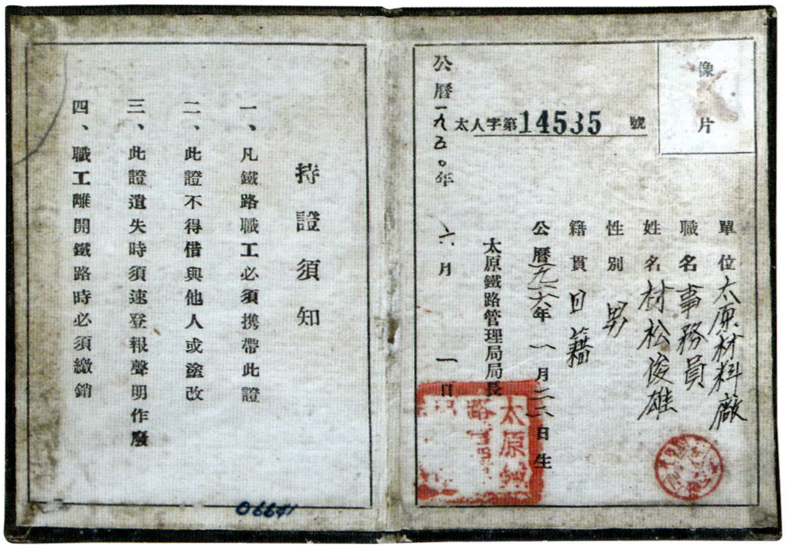

181 **铁路职工服务证（日籍员工）**

Service Card of Staffs（Japanese Staffs）

182 **铁路职工服务证封皮**

Protecting Case of Staffs' Service Card

183 **铁路职工工作证**

Employment Certificate of Railway Staffs

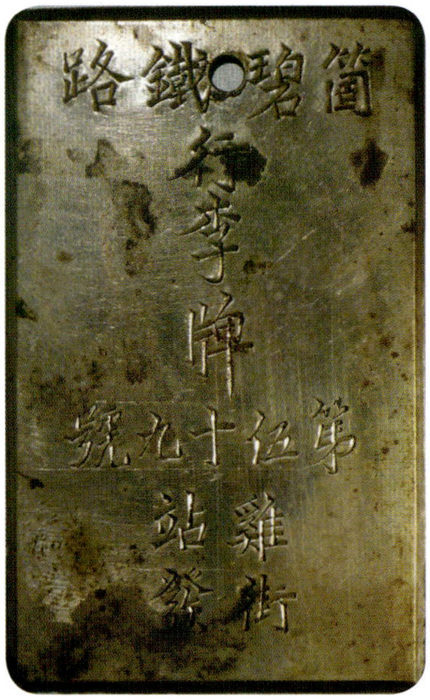

184 个碧石铁路托运行李牌（三级文物）

Luggage Tag of Gejiu-Bisezhai-Shiping Railway Company（National Grade-three Cultural Relic）

185 1943年交通火车乘车证（三级文物）

The Boarding Card of Communications Ministry in 1943（National Grade-three Cultural Relic）

186 乘车证（民国二十六年造）（三级文物）

Boarding Card（National Grade-three Cultural Relic）

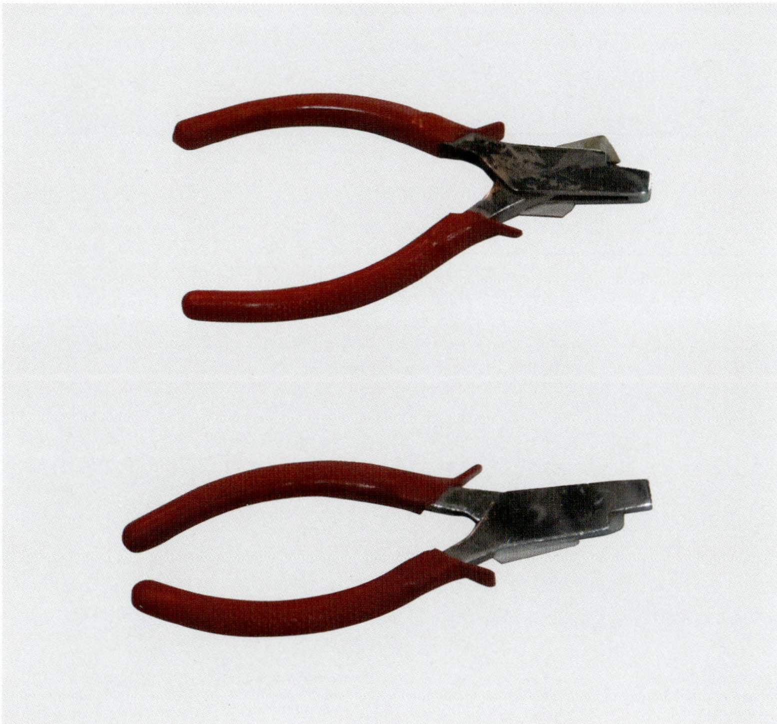

187 检票钳

Ticket Check Pliers

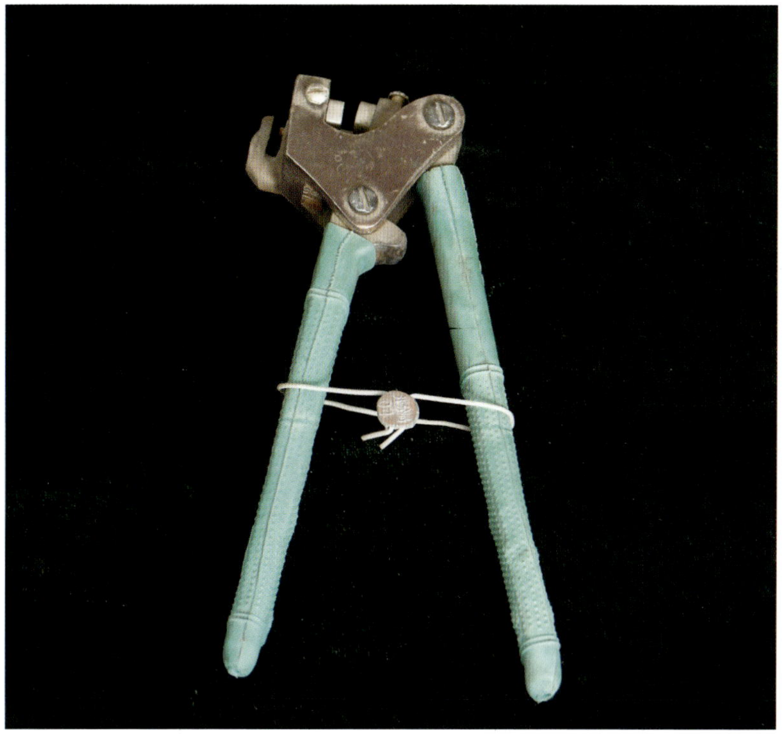

188 铅封钳

Lead Sealing Pliers

189 货运章

Freight Stamp

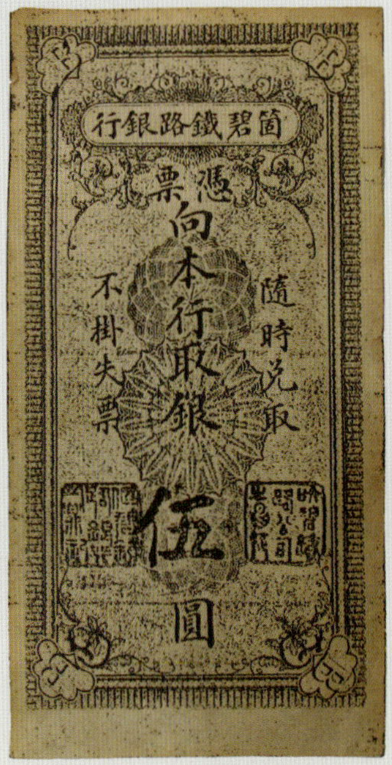

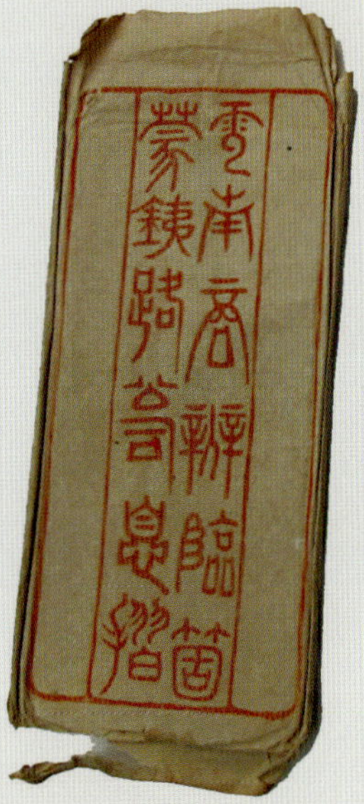

Since France grabbed the rights of railway construction and operation, Yunnan market was flooded with different silver dollars, copper coins and bills issued by France, Vietnam, Chinese governments and local government of Yunnan, making local economy and finance in great disorder. Until 1919, on their own land, the Yunnan people built and operated the inch-gauge railway that was totally supported and managed by private entrepreneurs. They founded Gejiu-Bisezhai-Shiping Railway Bank, issuing railway bonds and stocks to raise social money. This example of private industrialists and businessmen's success in applying western market economy and finance to the development of railway career embodied the forward-looking spirit, pragmatic innovation and patriotism of the Yunnan people.

第8章 钱币债券

Article eighth

Currencies and Debentures

在法国人攫取筑路权和经营权的滇越铁路上，原来充斥着法国、越南、中国中央政府和云南地方政府发行的各种银圆、铜币、纸钞等，一度造成地方经济和金融的动荡。1919年，云南人为在自己的乡土上修筑和运营民资民办民营的寸轨小铁路，创立了个碧石铁路银行，自主发行铁路银行券和股票，吸纳社会资本，认购铁路股份。这是云南工商业者运用西方市场经济手段和金融操作方式来发展铁路的实例，体现了云南人民学习先进、发展实业、爱国救乡的首创精神。

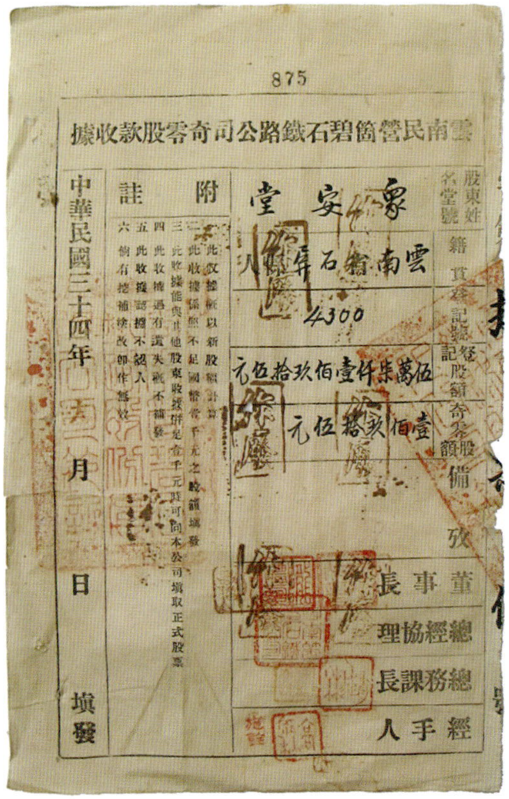
875

雲南民營個碧石鐵路公司奇零股款收據

股東姓名堂號

籍貫

附註

董事長

總協理

總務課長

經手人

中華民國三十四年 月 日 填發

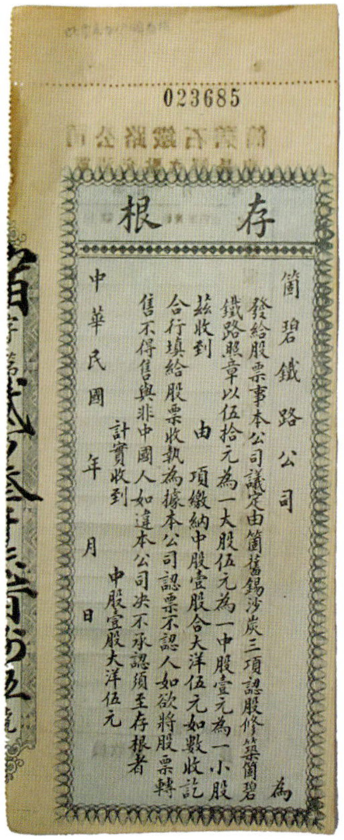
023685

存根

箇碧鐵路公司 為發給股票事本公司議定由箇舊錫沙炭三項認股修築箇碧鐵路股章以伍拾元為一大股伍元為一中股壹元為一小股 茲收到 由 項繳納中股壹股合大洋伍元如數收訖合行填給股票收執為據本公司認票不認人如欲將股票轉售不得售與非中國人如違本公司決不承認須至存根者

計實收到 中股壹股大洋伍元

中華民國 年 月 日

190 个碧铁路公司奇零股款收据

Sporadic Receipt for Share Issued by Gejiu–Bisezhai Railway Company

191 个碧铁路1912年股票存根

Stock Stub of Gejiu–Bisezhai Railway in 1912

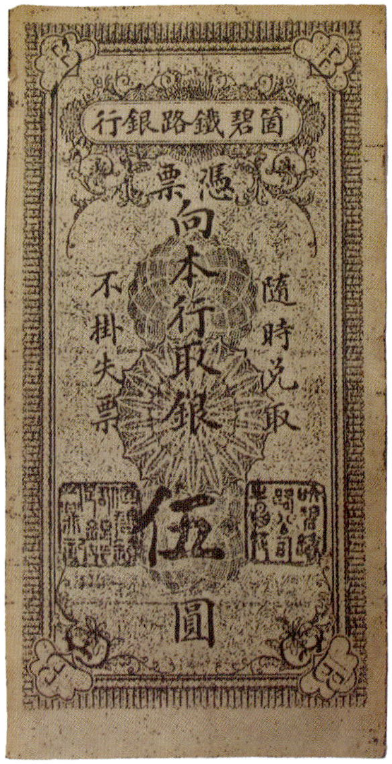
箇碧鐵路銀行

憑票向本行取銀

隨時兌取

不掛失票

伍圓

192 个碧铁路银行券

Bank Notes Issued by Gejiu–Bisezhai Railway Bank

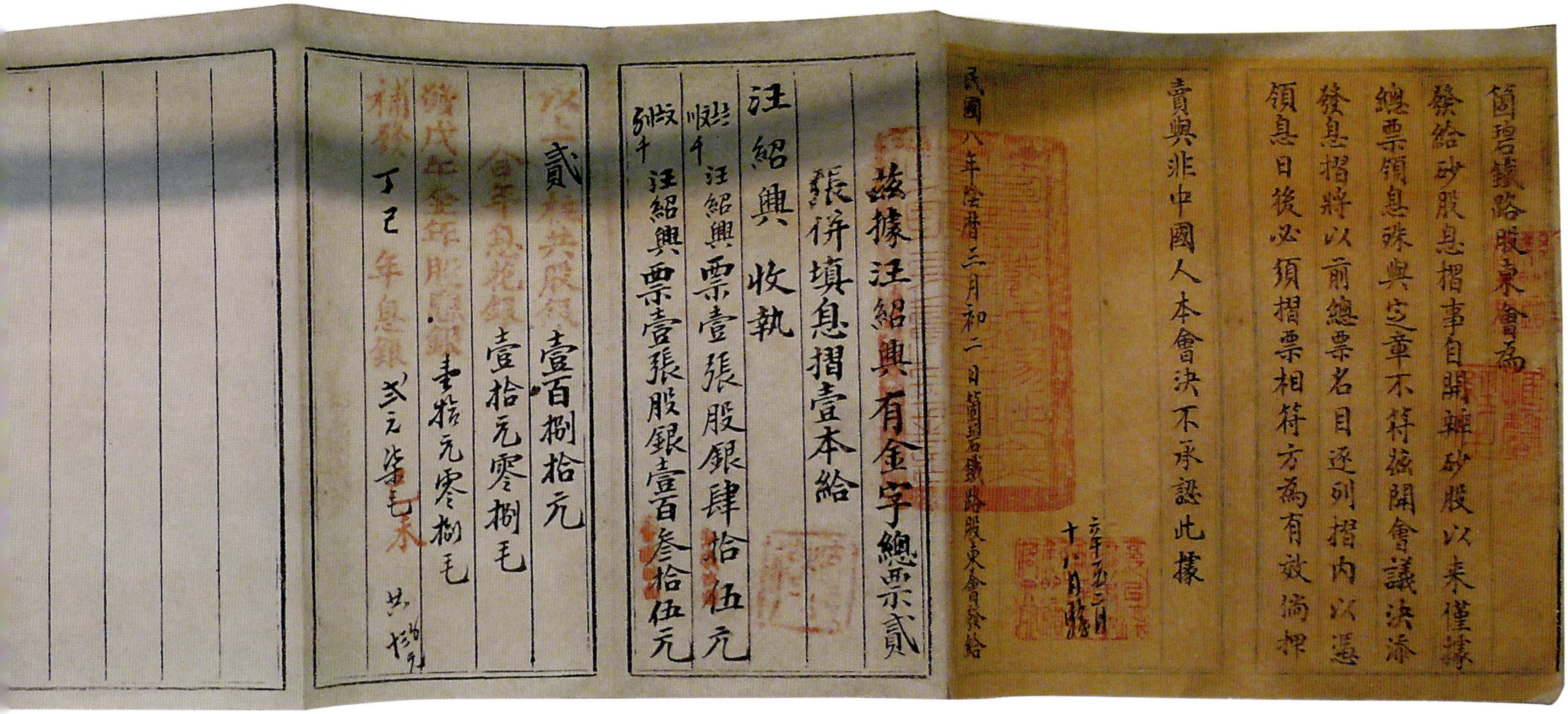

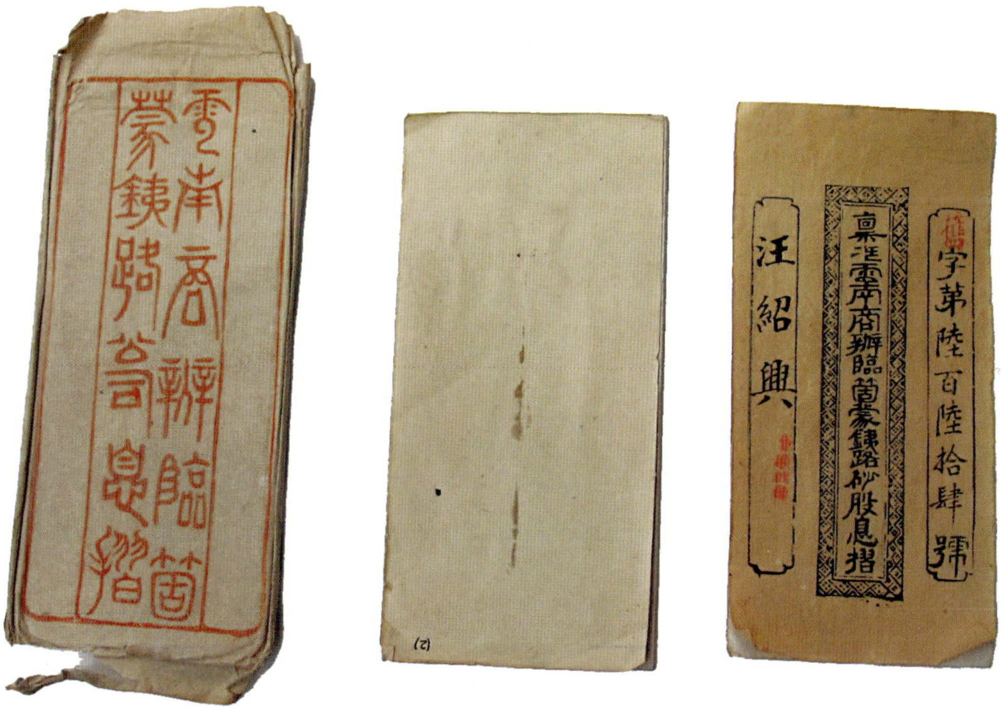

193 个碧铁路股票持股凭证

Share Certificate of Gejiu-Bisezhai Railway

194 临个蒙铁路股票红利凭证

Share Certificate of Cash Dividends Issued by Jianshui-Gejiu-Mengzi Railway

195 纸币

Paper Currency

196 法营时期所用货币

Coin Used in 1910~1945（Under France's Operation)

197 民国半圆钱币

Semicircle Coins Used in the Republic of China

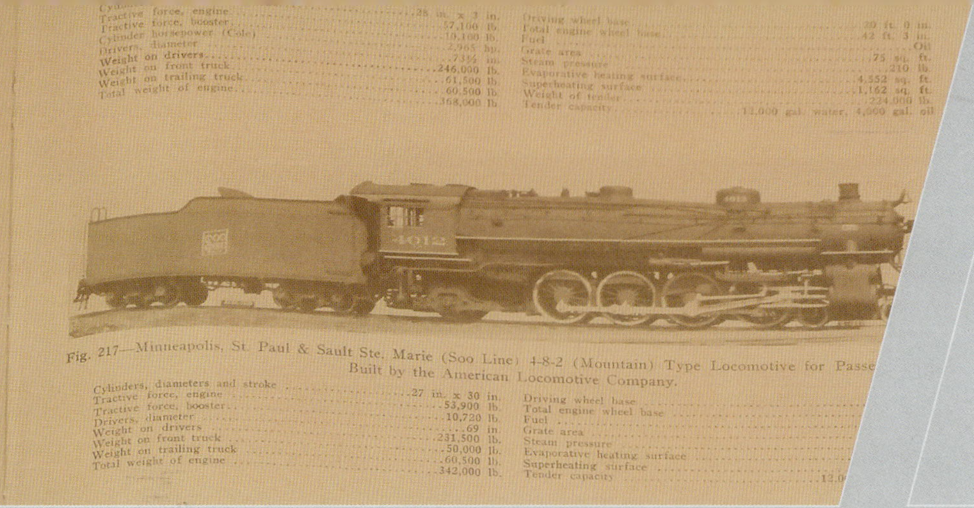
Fig. 217—Minneapolis, St. Paul & Sault Ste. Marie (Soo Line) 4-8-2 (Mountain) Type Locomotive for Passe
Built by the American Locomotive Company.

滇越鐵路
Le Chemin de Fer du YUNNAN
Avril 1910
MECHANICAL ENGINEERS' HANDBOOK
LIONEL S. MARKS Editor-in-Chief
Second Edition
McGRAW-HILL BOOK COMPANY
WALWORTH
Number 88
The Westinghouse Air Brake Company
American Railway Association
MANUAL

第9章

Article ninth

典籍章制

Ancient Books and Records

在云南铁路百年发展的风雨历程中，积淀了大量关于铁路运输生产和运营管理的规章文献和典籍章制，还有公司章程、作业规定、文件报告、技术书籍、铁道年鉴等弥足珍贵的历史资料，将其收集保存并整理展示，是铁路博物馆传承历史和弘扬文化的使命。

During development of one hundred years, a large number of ancient books and records about transportation production and operational management remained. These documents contain a plenty of historic information such as articles of company, regulations of activities, reports, technology books and railway almanacs. It is mission for the museum to keep them protected and displayed in order to tell the history and carry forward culture.

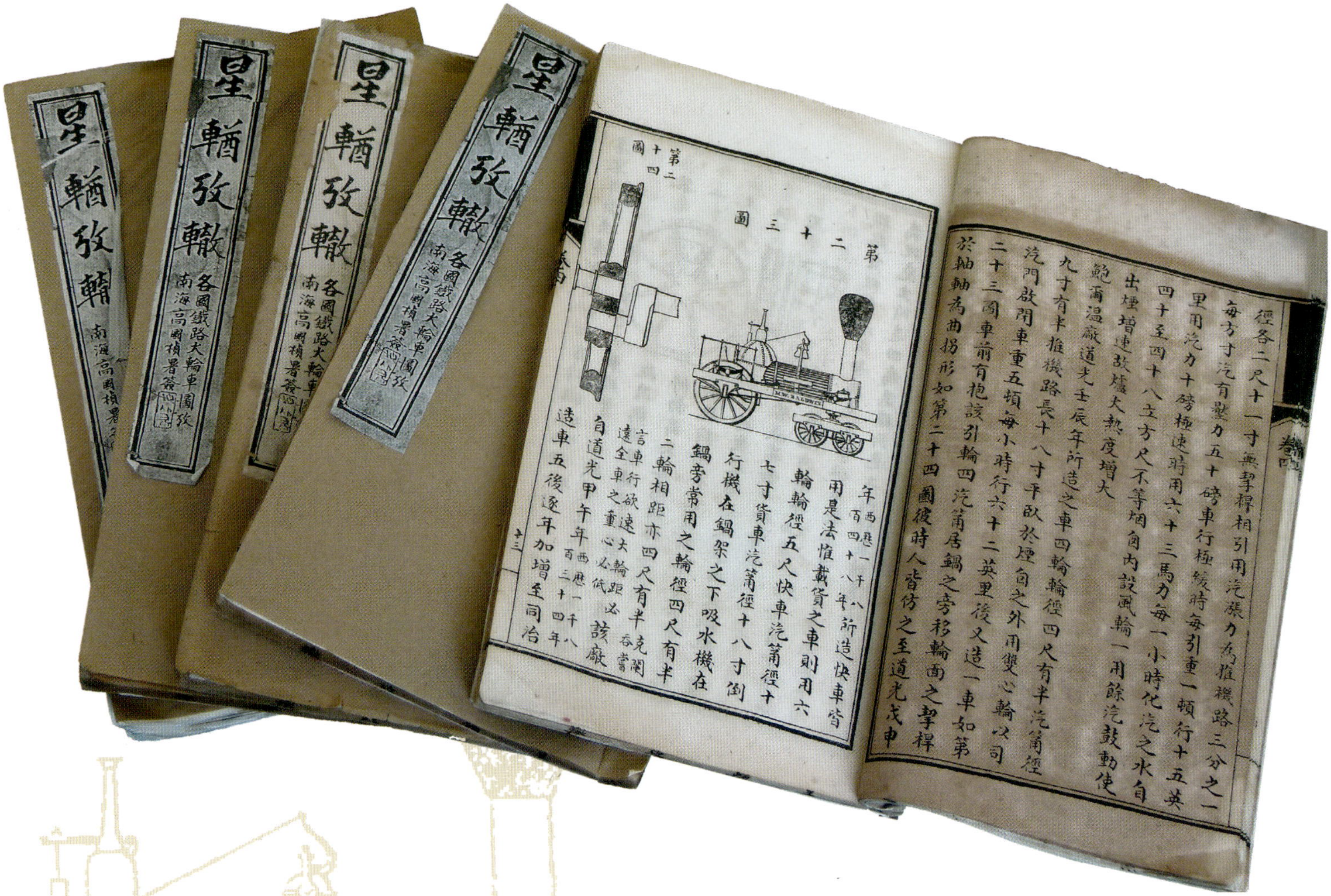

198《星輶考辙—各国铁路火轮车图考》(清代)

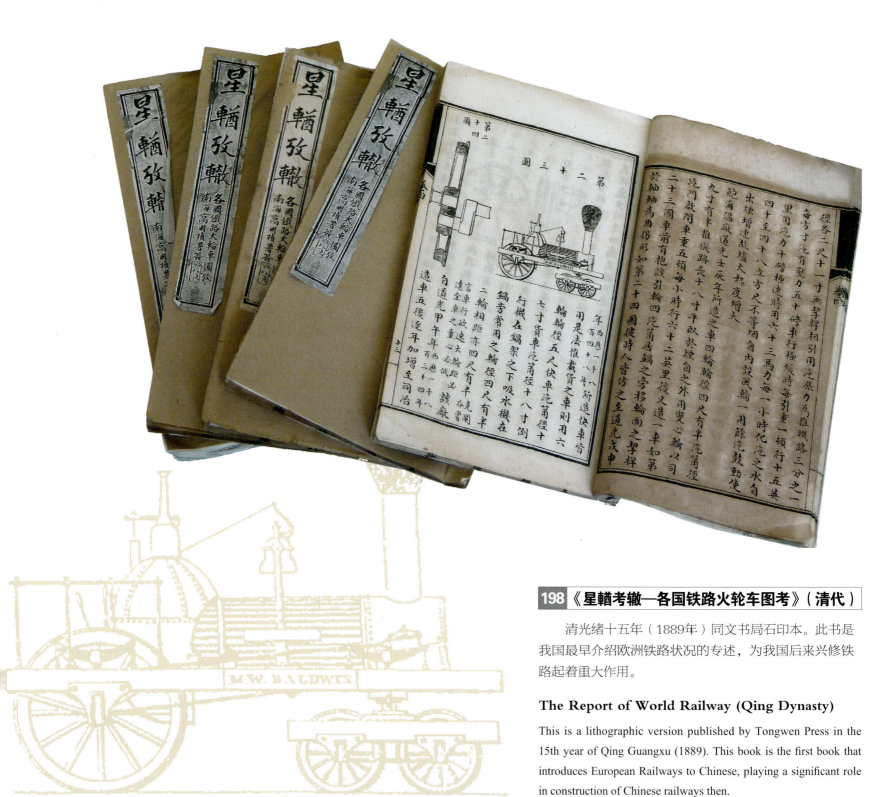

清光绪十五年(1889年)同文书局石印本。此书是我国最早介绍欧洲铁路状况的专述,为我国后来兴修铁路起着重大作用。

The Report of World Railway (Qing Dynasty)

This is a lithographic version published by Tongwen Press in the 15th year of Qing Guangxu (1889). This book is the first book that introduces European Railways to Chinese, playing a significant role in construction of Chinese railways then.

199 外文铁路技术手册

The Technical Handbook of Railways in Foreign Languages

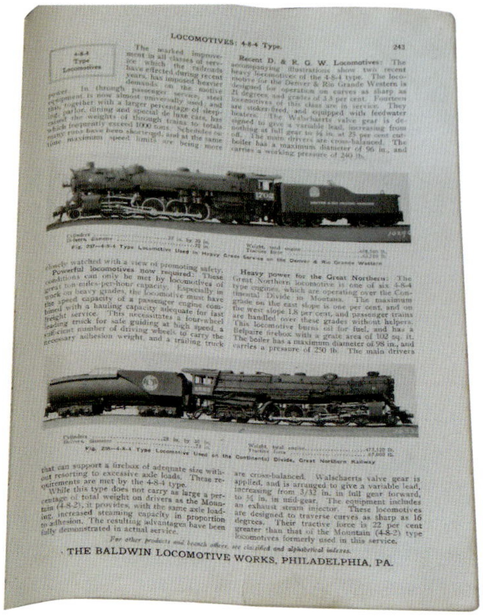

200《美国蒸汽机车大全》

Complete Collection of Steam Locomotives of U.S.A in 19th Century

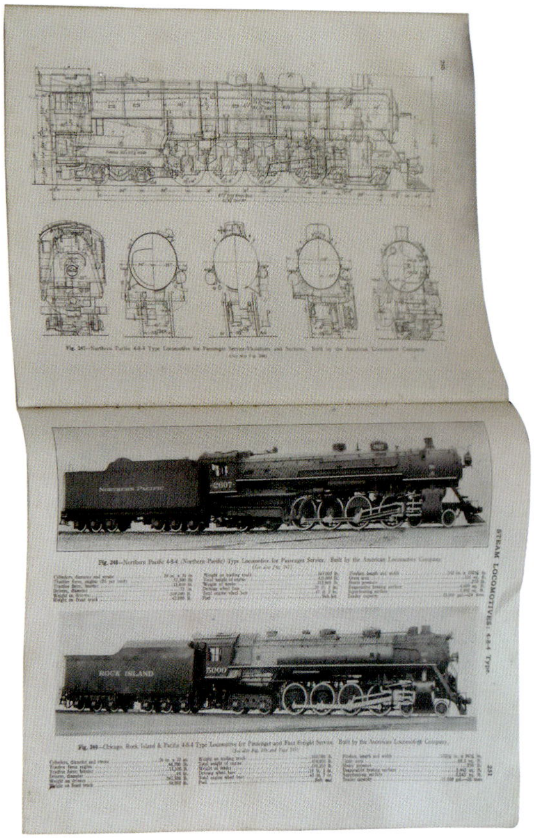

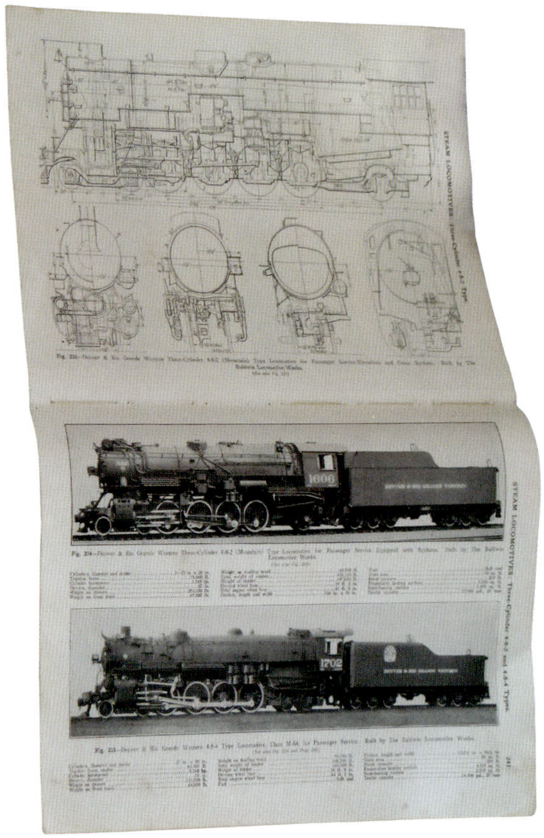

STEAM LOCOMOTIVES: 4-6-2 Type.
237

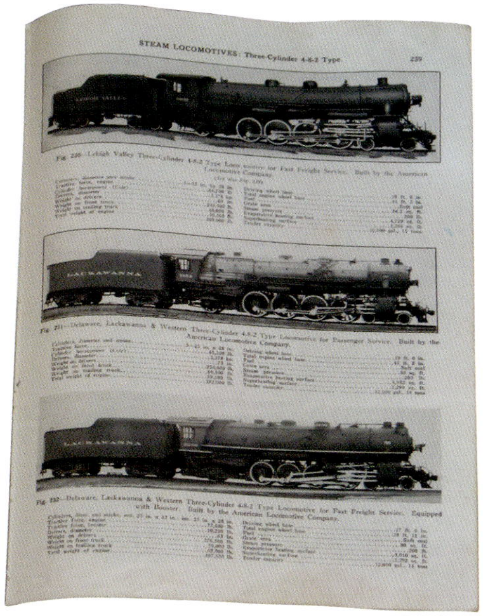
STEAM LOCOMOTIVES: Three-Cylinder 4-6-2 Type.
239

STEAM LOCOMOTIVES: 4-8-4 Type.
245

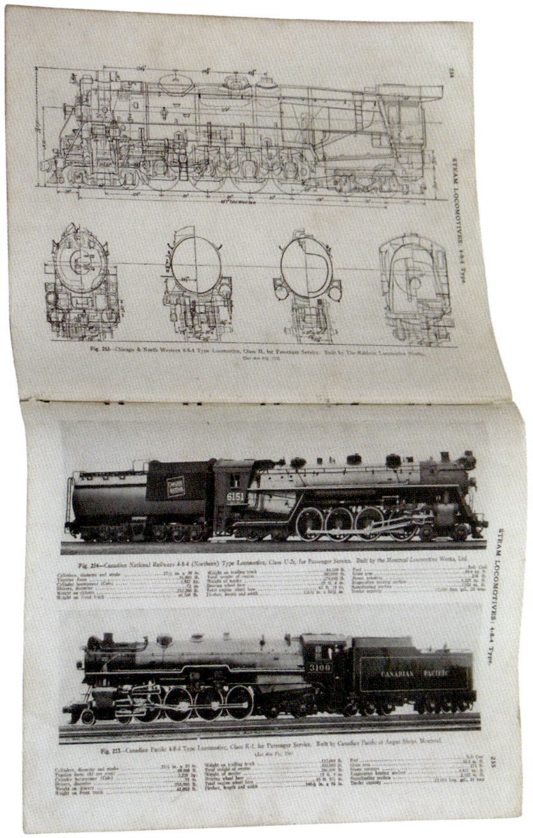

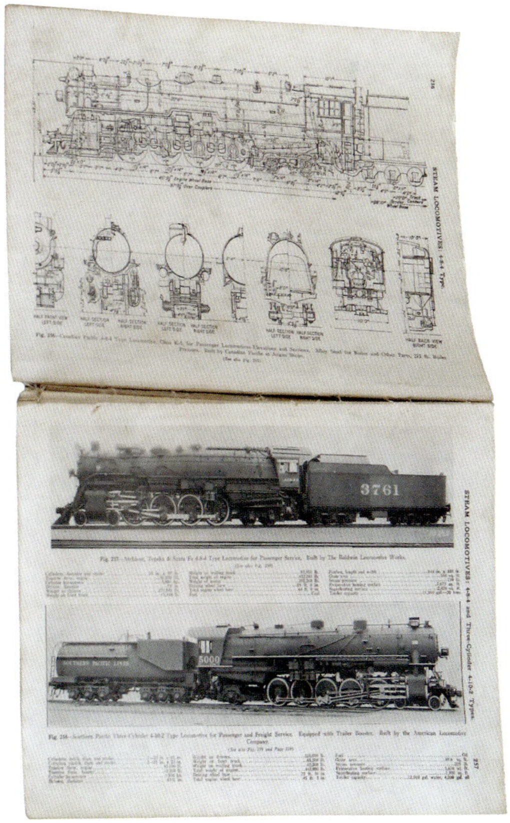

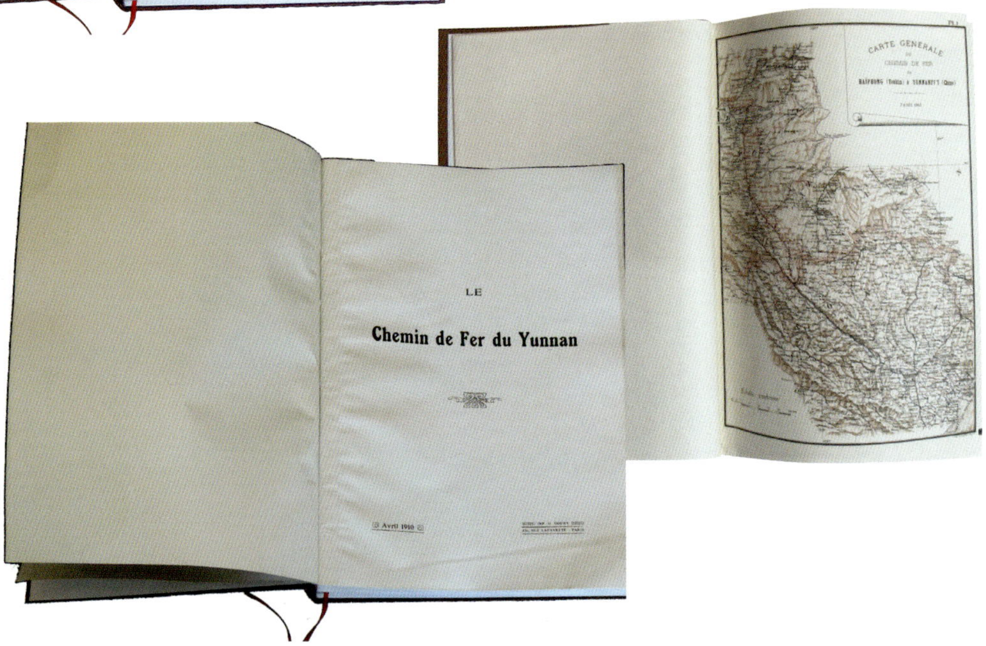

201 《滇越铁路》上、下册

年代：1910年　　出版：法国巴黎

An Album of Yunnan–Vietnam Railway

Year: 1910　　Published by Paris, France

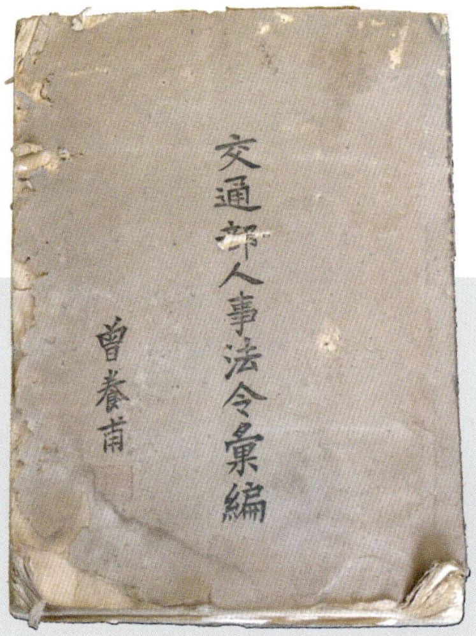

202 《交通部人事法令汇编》

年代：1930年

Regulations of Personnel by Communication Ministry

Year: 1930

203《铁道年鉴》

年代：1930年

The Railway Yearbook

Year: 1930

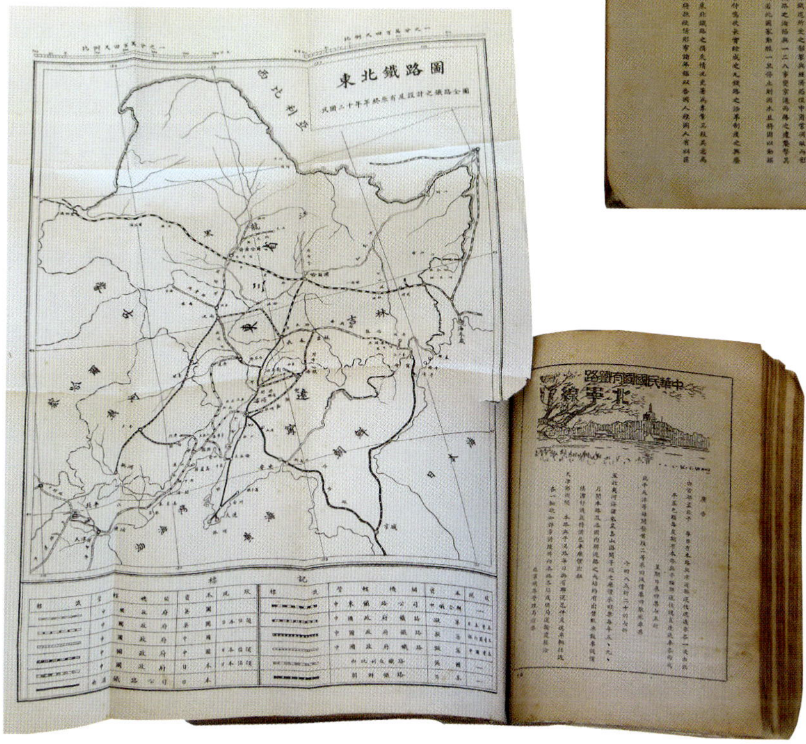

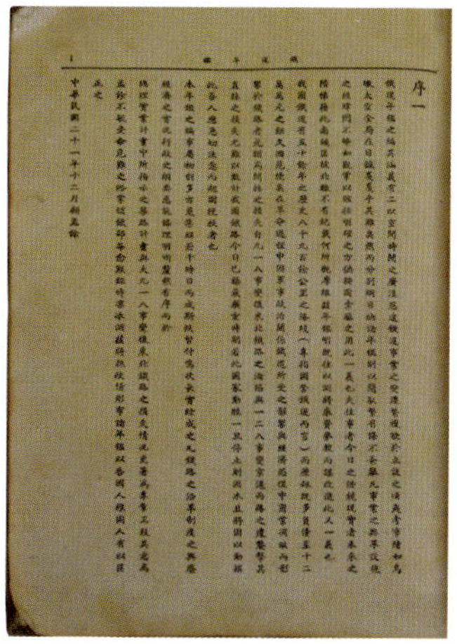

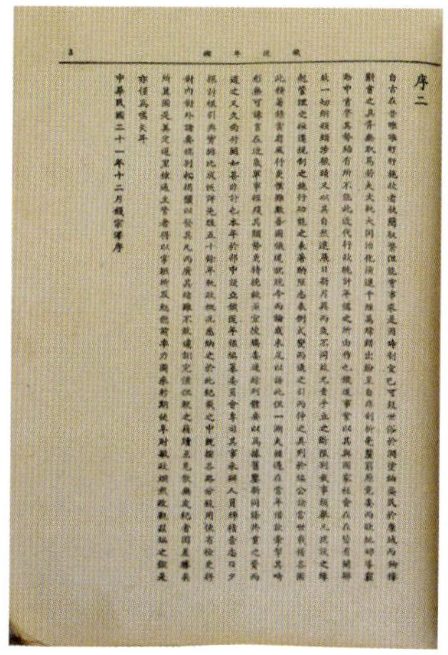

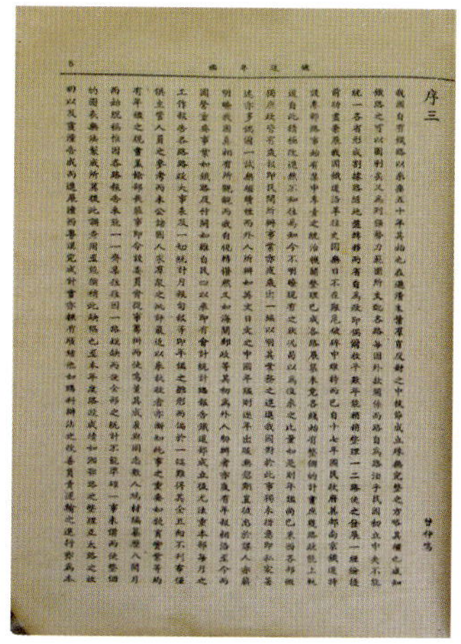

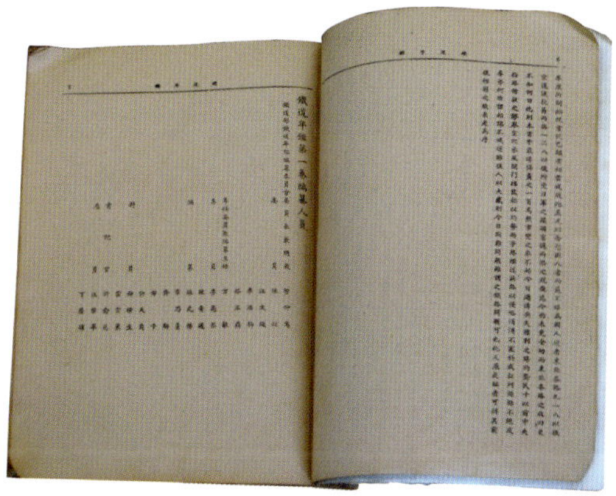

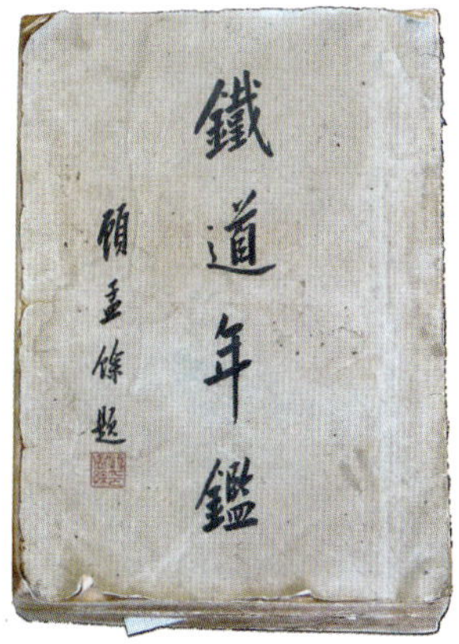

204 民国时期编写的铁道年鉴（第三卷）

1936年，南京出版。

The Railway Yearbook Compiled in the Period of the Republic of China

Published by Nanjing, 1936

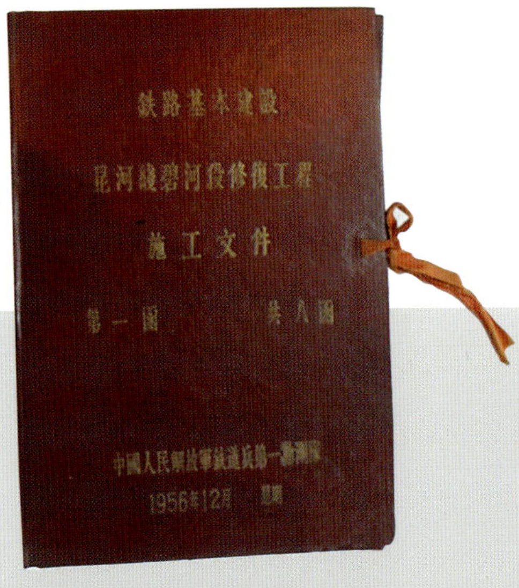

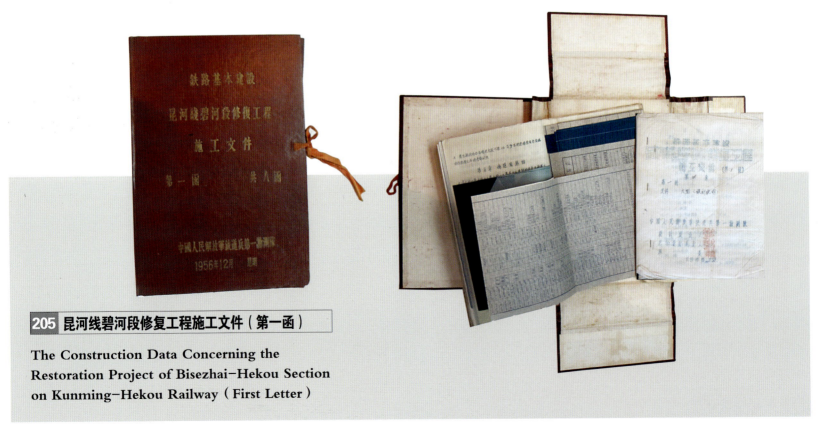

205 昆河线碧河段修复工程施工文件（第一函）

The Construction Data Concerning the Restoration Project of Bisezhai–Hekou Section on Kunming–Hekou Railway（First Letter）

206 滇缅铁路勘察报告书

年代：1939年

The Survey and Investigation Reports of Yunnan-Myanmar Railway

Year: 1939

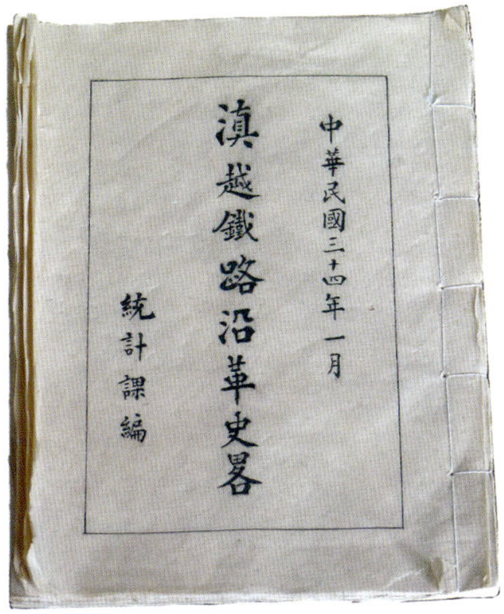

207 《滇越铁路沿革史略》

年代：1945年

The Brief History of Yunnan-Vietnam Railway

Year: 1945

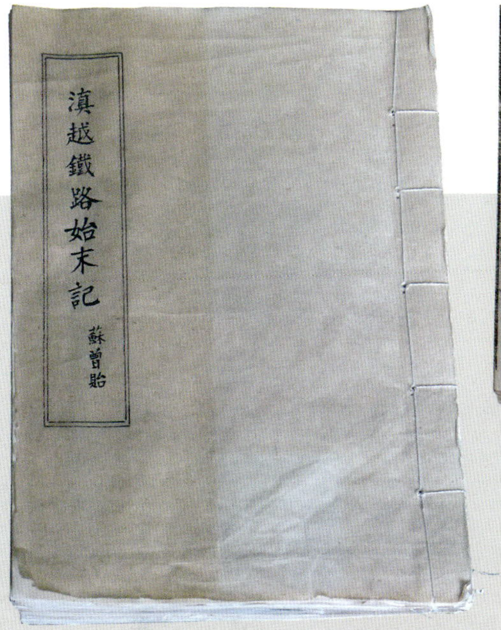

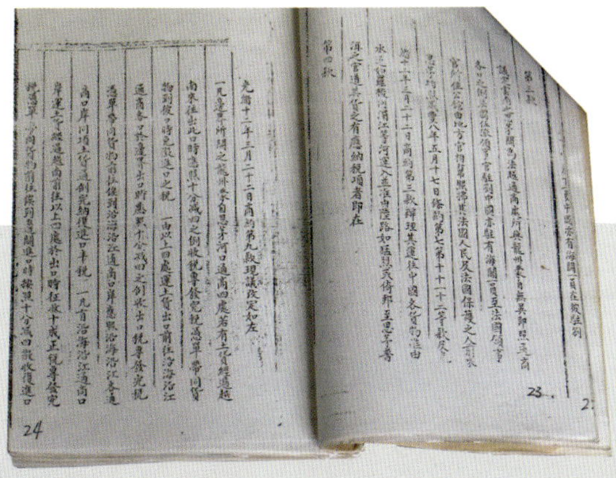

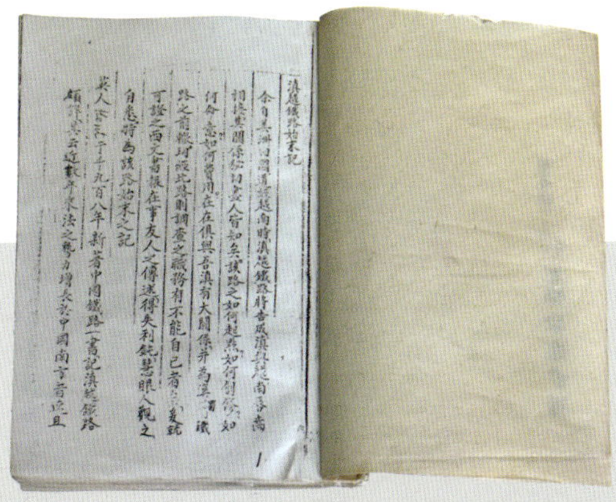

208 滇越铁路始末记

The History of Yunnan-Vietnam Railway

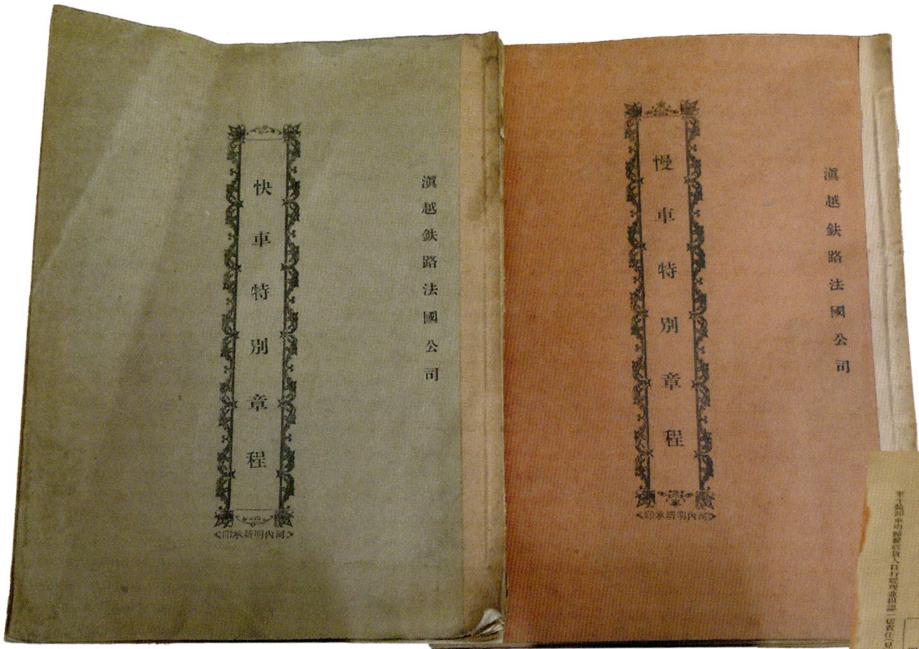

209 滇越铁路慢车特别章程

The Special Regulation of Slow Train of Yunnan-Vietnam Railway

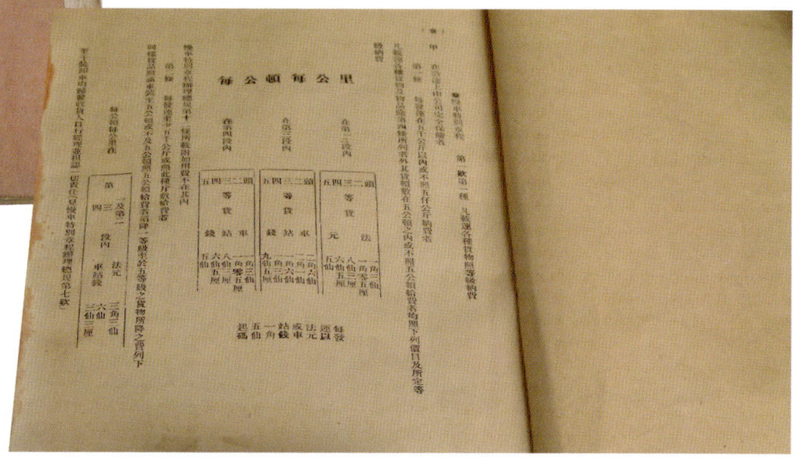

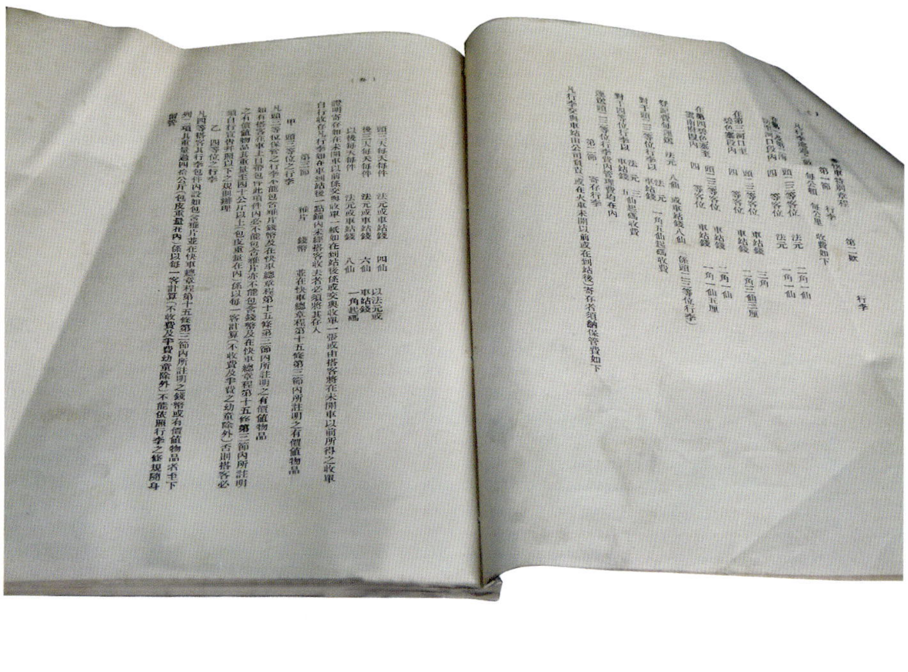

210 滇越铁路快车特别章程

The Special Regulation of Express Train of Yunnan-Vietnam Railway

211 滇越铁路列车时刻表

Train Schedule of Yunnan-Vietnam Railway

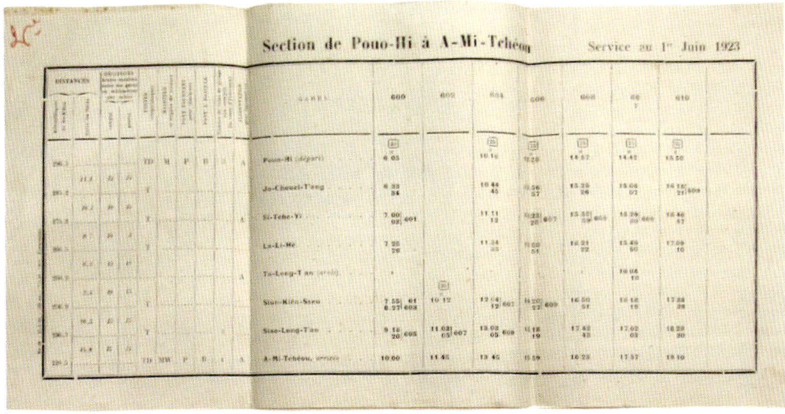

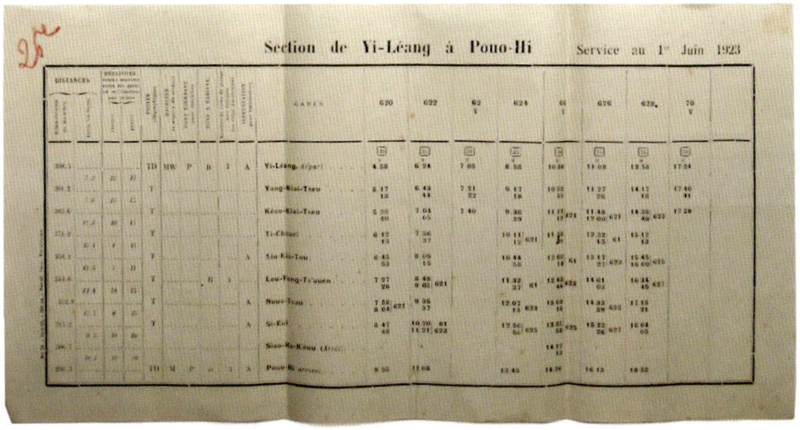

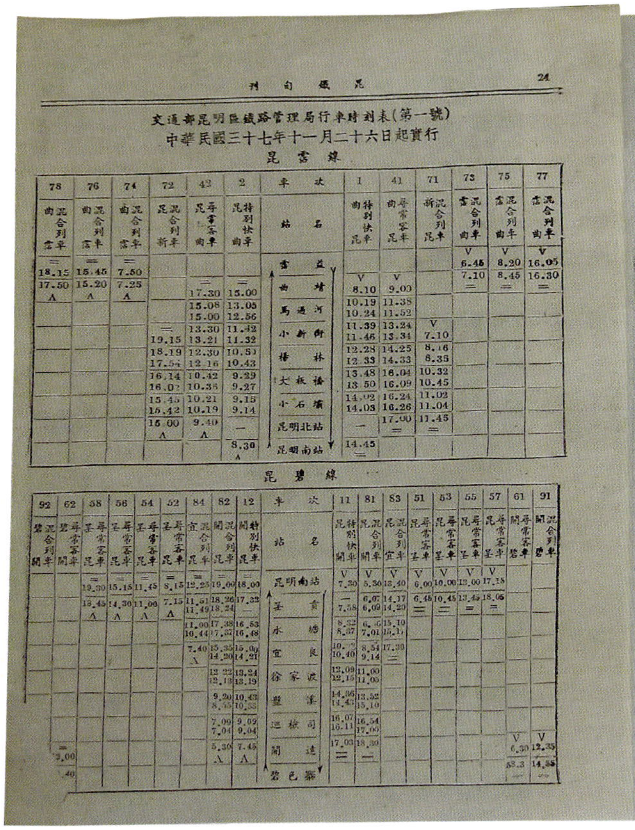

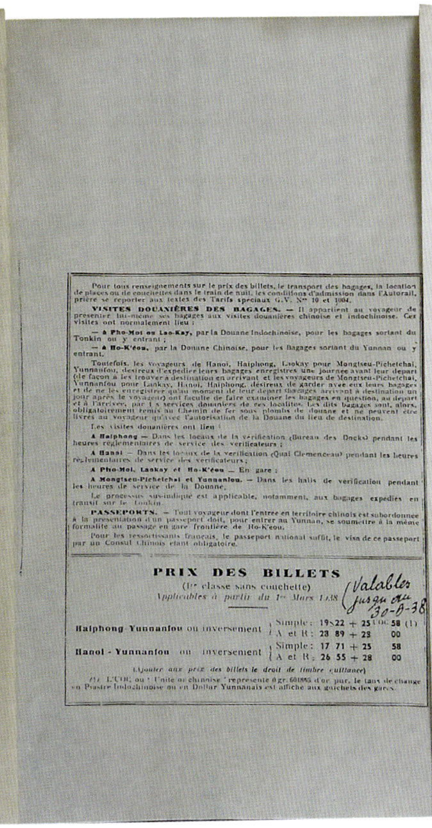

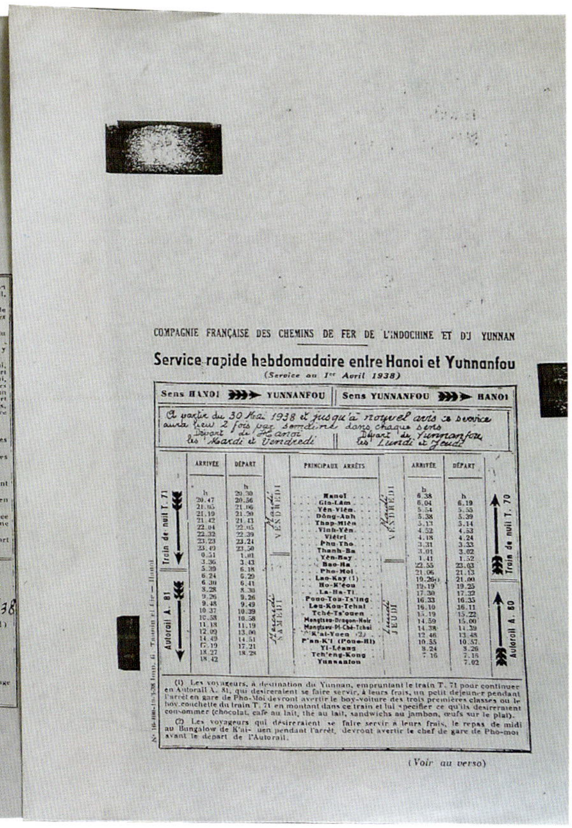

212 线路改造的设计文件

Design of Track Remodelling

213 滇越铁路碧河段修复工程设计资料

年代：1956年

Design Concerning the Restoration Project of Bisezhai–Hekou Section on Yunnan–Vietnam Railway

Year: 1956

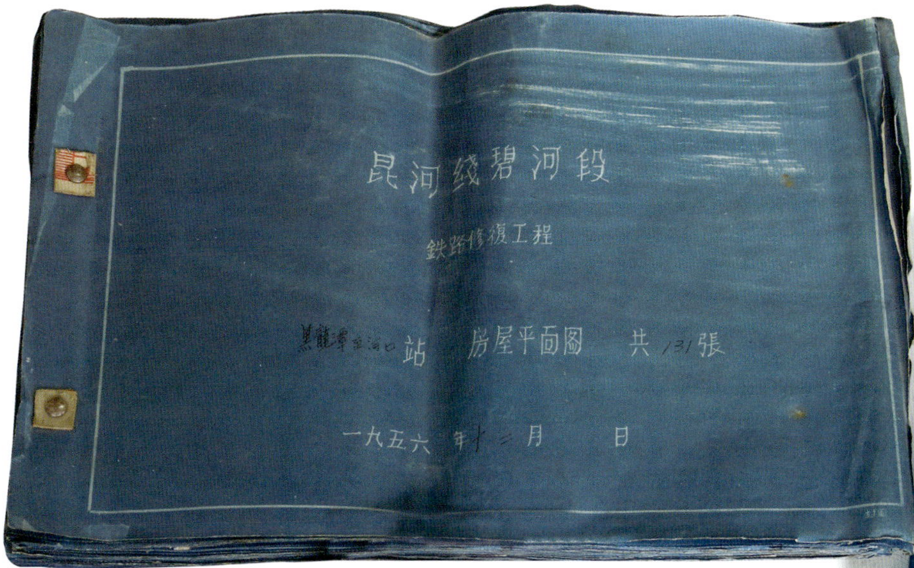

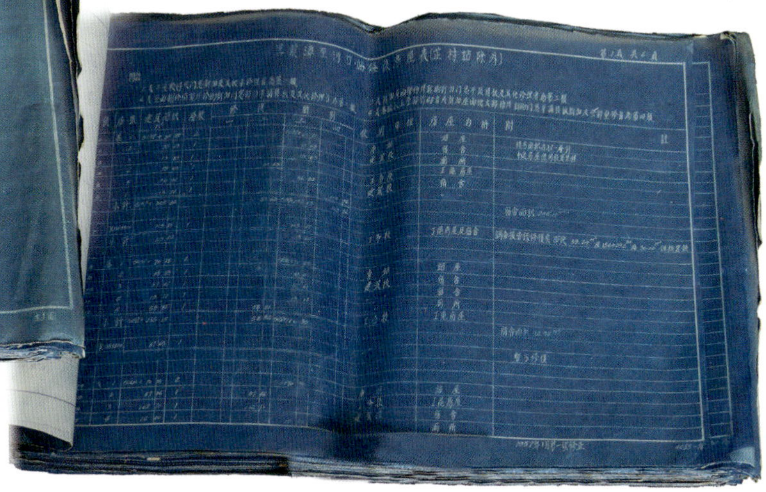

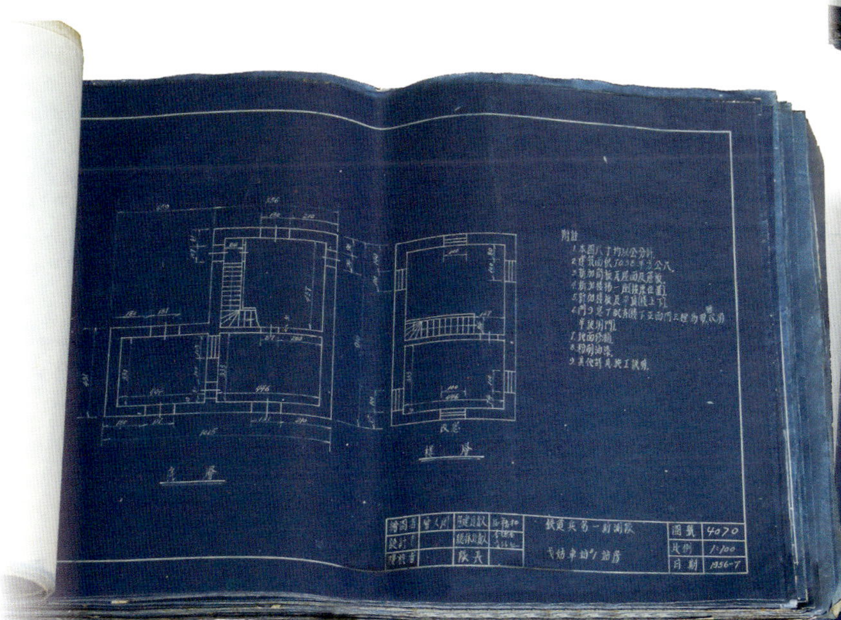

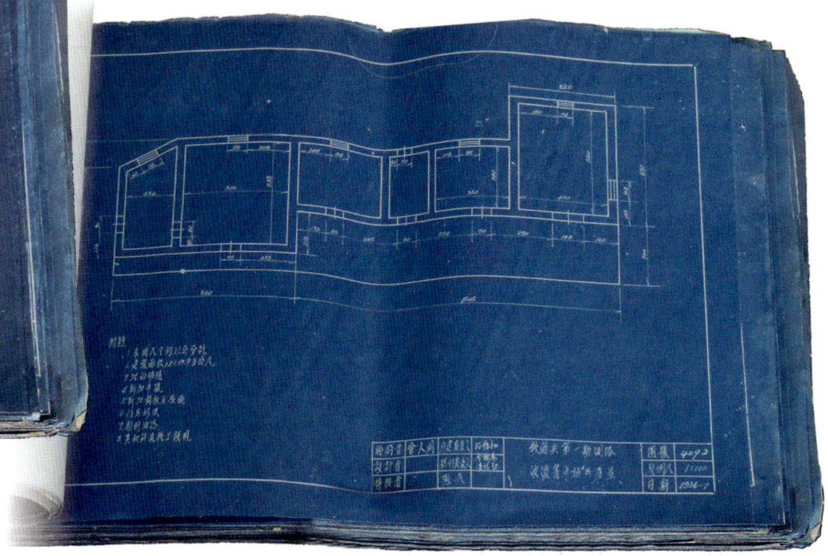

214 云南民营个碧石铁路股份有限公司新组董事会宣言

Declaration of the Newly Established Boarding of Directors of Gejiu-Bisezhai-Shiping Railway (Ltd), a Private company of Yunnan

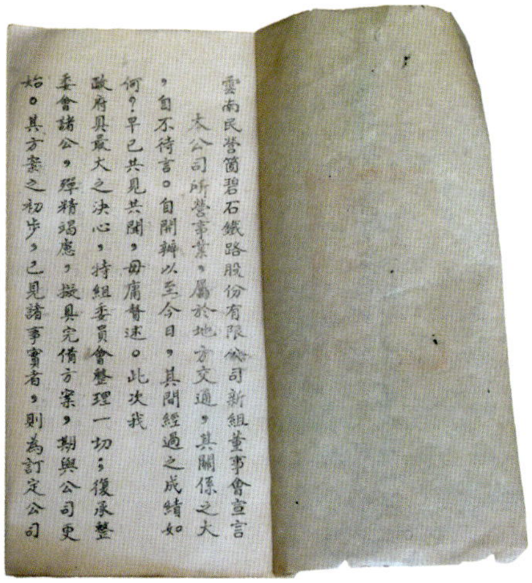

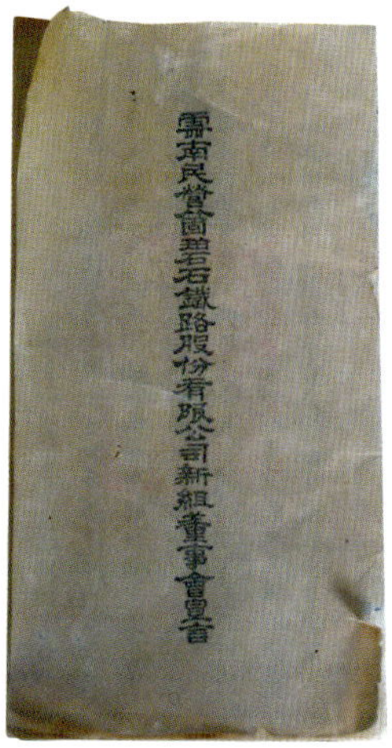

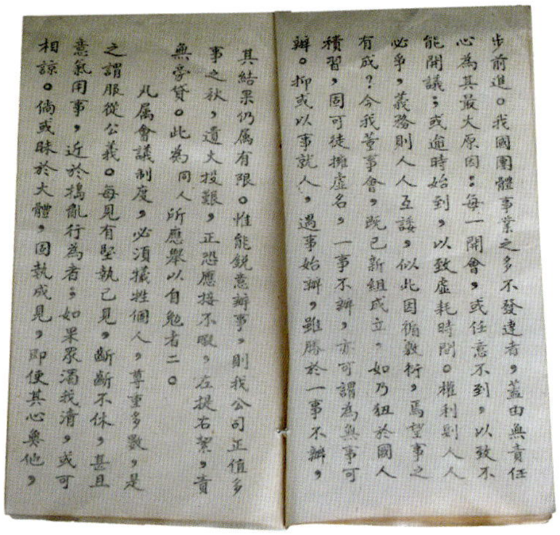

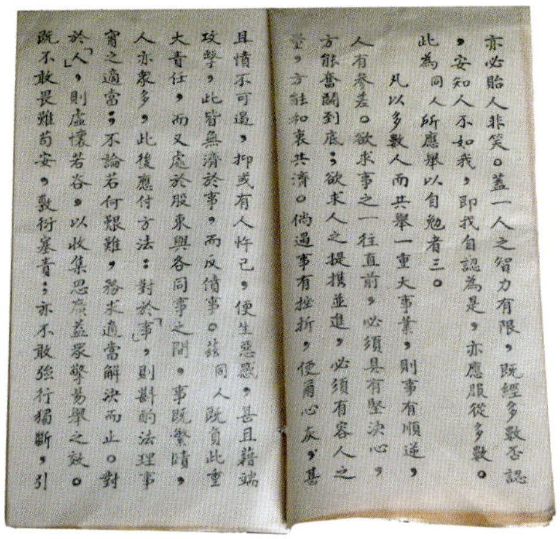

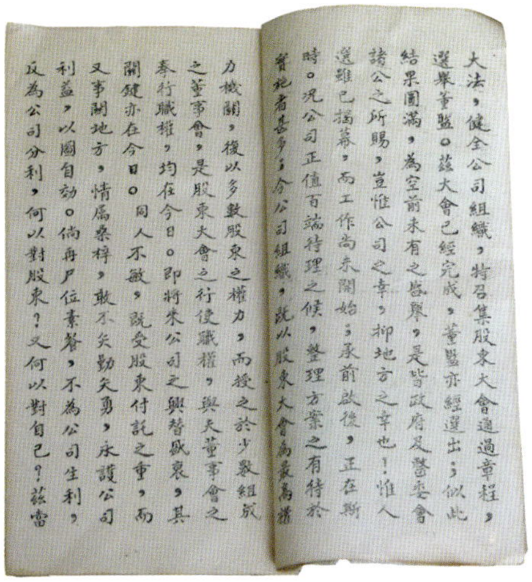

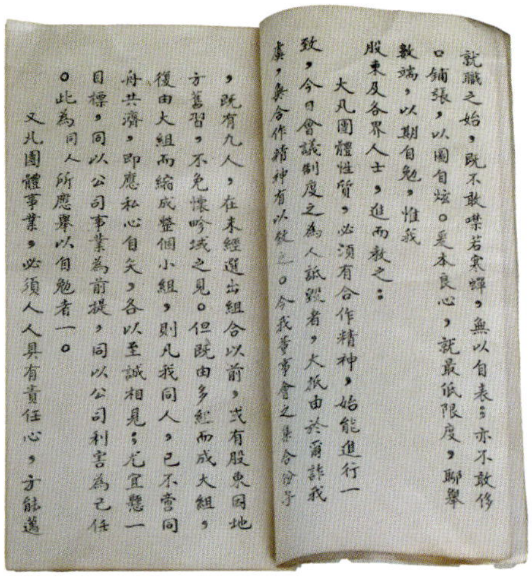

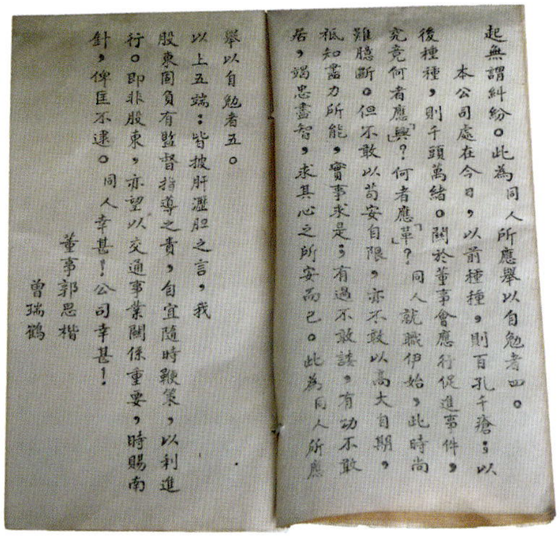

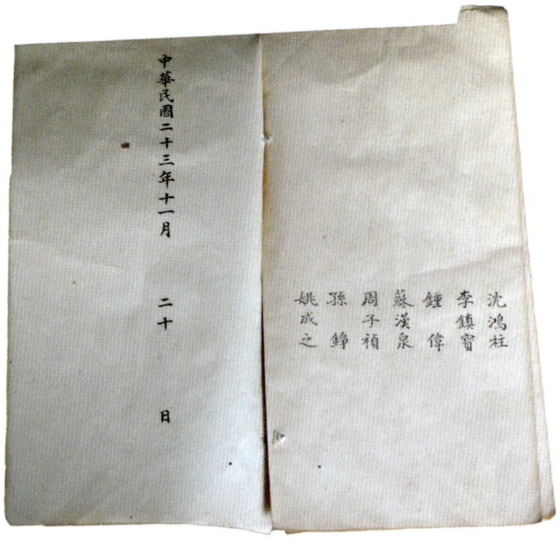

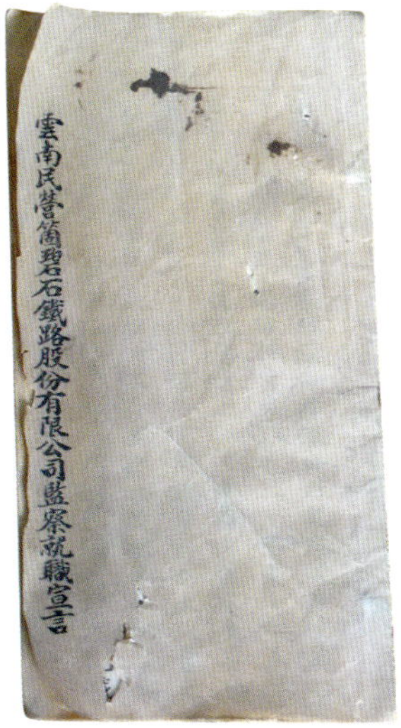

雲南民營箇碧石鐵路股份有限公司監察就職宣言

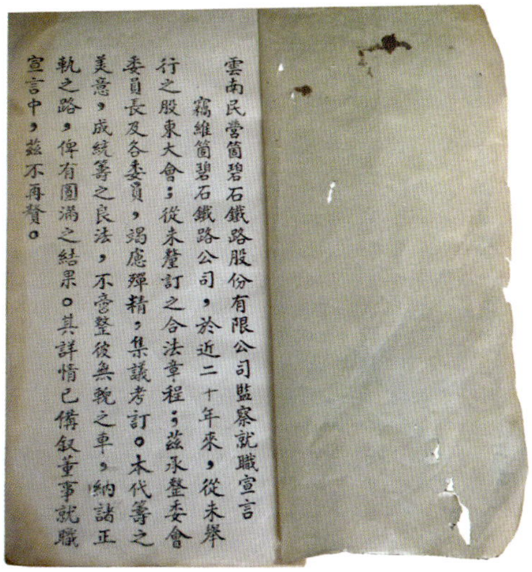

雲南民營箇碧石鐵路股份有限公司監察就職宣言

竊維箇碧石鐵路公司，於近二十年來，從未舉行之股東大會；從未釐訂之合法章程；茲承釐委會委員長及各委員，竭慮殫精，集議考訂。本代籌之美意，成統籌之良法，不啻登彼無軌之車，納諸正軌之路，俾有圓滿之結果。其詳情已備敘董事就職宣言中，茲不再贅。

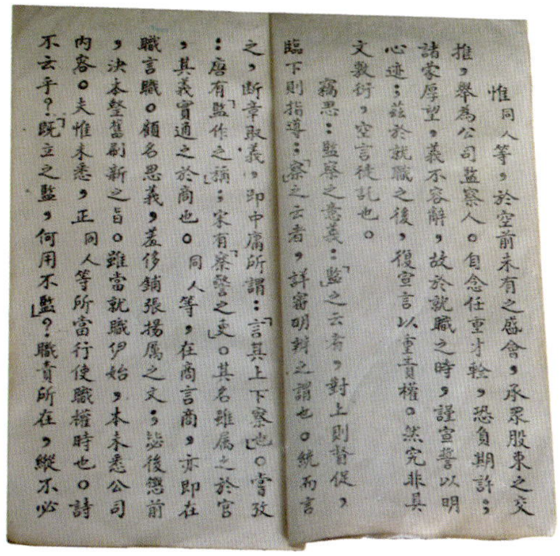

惟同人等，於空前未有之盛會，承眾股東之交推，舉為公司監察人。自念任重才輕，恐負期許；諸家厚望，義不容辭，故於就職之時，謹宣誓以明心迹；茲於就職之後，復宣言以重責權。然究非具文敷衍，空言徒託也。

竊思：監察之意義：「監」之云者，對上則督促，臨下則指導；「察」之云者，詳審明辨之謂也。統而言之，斷章取義，即中庸所謂：「言其上下察也」。嘗致：唐有「監作之稱」；宋有「察警之吏」。其名雖屬之於官，其義實通之於商也。同人等，在商言商，亦即在職言職。顧名思義，蓋彷鋪張揚厲之文；懲後毖前，決本整舊刷新之旨。雖當就職伊始，本未悉公司內容。夫惟未悉，正同人等所當行使職權時也。詩不云乎？「既立之監」，何用不「監」？職責所在，縱不必

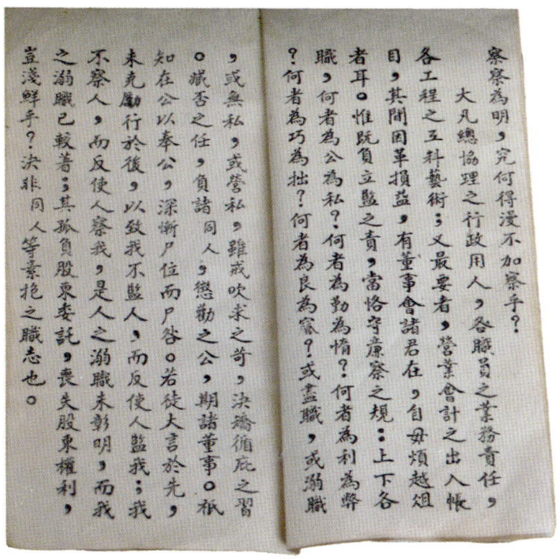

察察為明，究何得漫不加察乎？

大凡總協理之行政用人，各職員之業務責任，各工程之五料藝術；又最要者，營業會計之出入帳目，其間因革損益，有董事會諸君在，自毋煩越俎者耳。惟既負立監之責，當恪守廉察之規：上下各職，何者為公為私？何者為勤為惰？何者為利為弊？何者為巧為拙？何者為良為窳？或盡職，或溺職，或無私，或營私，雖戒吹求之苛，決矯循庇之習。臧否之任，負諸同人，懲勸之公，期諸董事。祇知在公以奉公，深慚尸位而尸咎。若徒大言於先，未克勵行於後，以致我不監人，而反使人監我；我不察人，而反使人察我，是人之溺職未彰明，而我之溺職已較著；其孤負股東委託，喪失股東權利，豈淺鮮乎？決非同人等素抱之職志也。

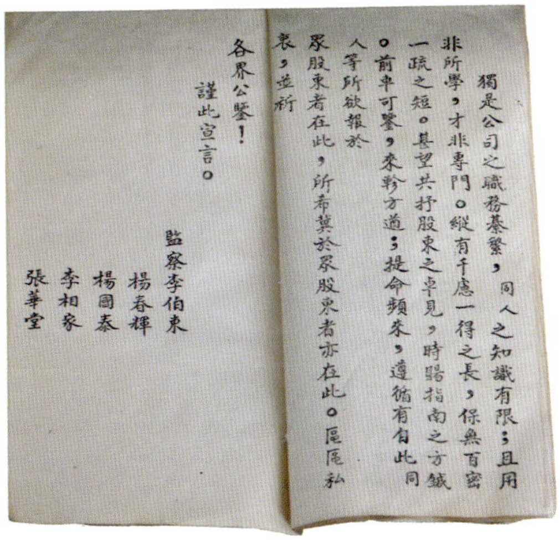

獨是公司之職務綦繁，同人之知識有限；且用非所學，才非專門。縱有千慮一得之長，保無百密一疏之短。甚望共抒股東之卓見，時賜指南之方鍼；前車可鑒，來軫方遒；提命頻來，遵循有自。此同人等所欲報於眾股東者在此，所希冀於眾股東者亦在此。區區私衷，並祈

各界公鑒！

謹此宣言。

監察李伯東
楊春輝
楊國泰
李相家
張華堂

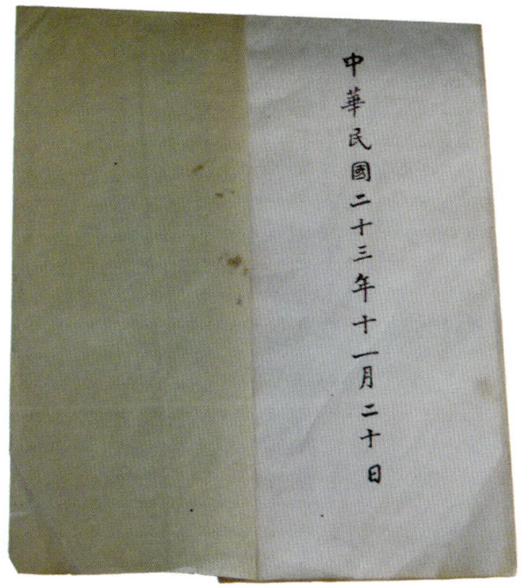

中華民國二十三年十一月二十日

215 云南民营个碧石铁路股份有限公司监察就职宣言

The Investigator's Oath of Office of Gejiu-Bisezhai-Shiping Railway (Ltd), a Private Company of Yunnan

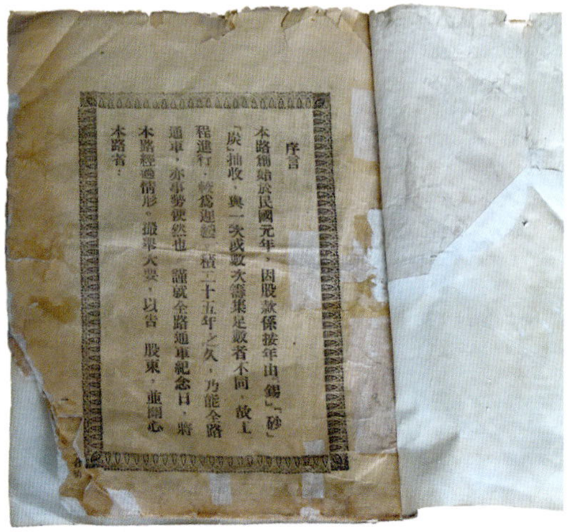

序言

本路籌始於民國元年，因股款係按年由「錫」「砂」「炭」抽收，與一次或數次籌集足數者不同，故工程進行，較爲遲緩，積三十五年之久，乃能全路通車，亦事勢使然也。謹就全路通車紀念日，將本路經過情形，撮舉大要，以告 股東，並關心本路者。

216 个碧石铁路全路通车纪念刊

Memorial Volume for the Opening of Gejiu-Bisezhai-Shiping Railway

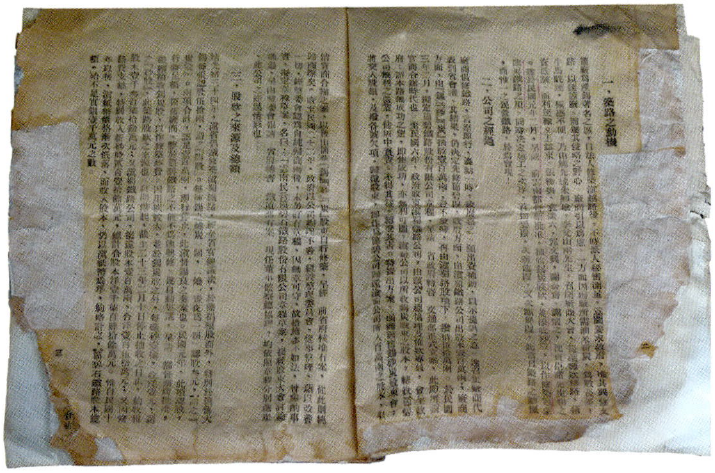

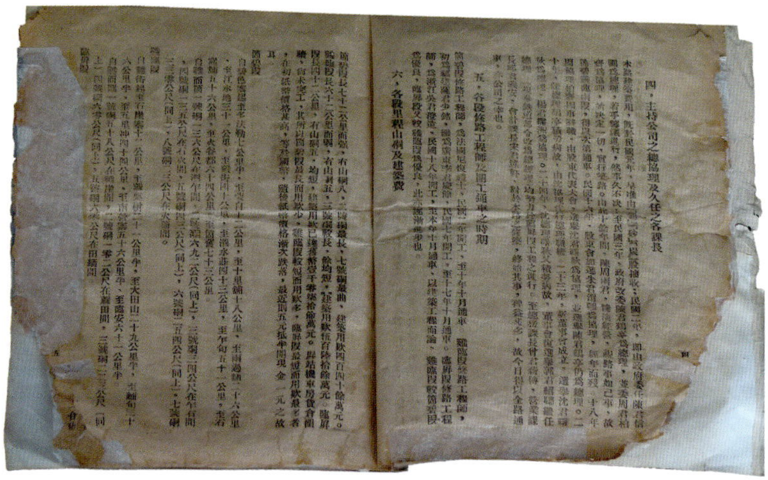

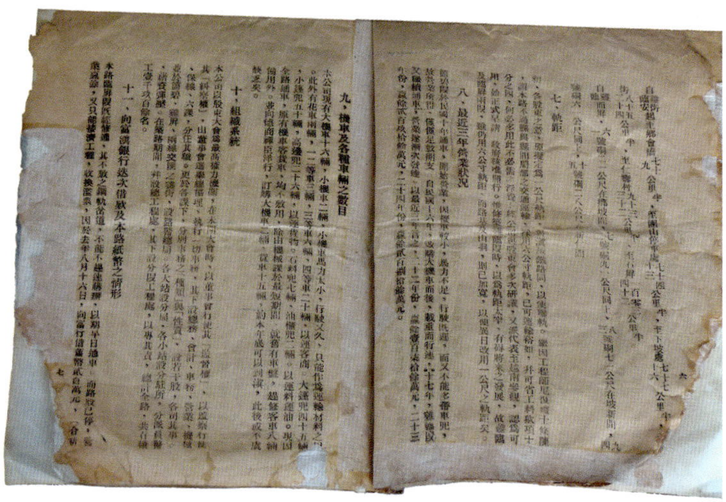

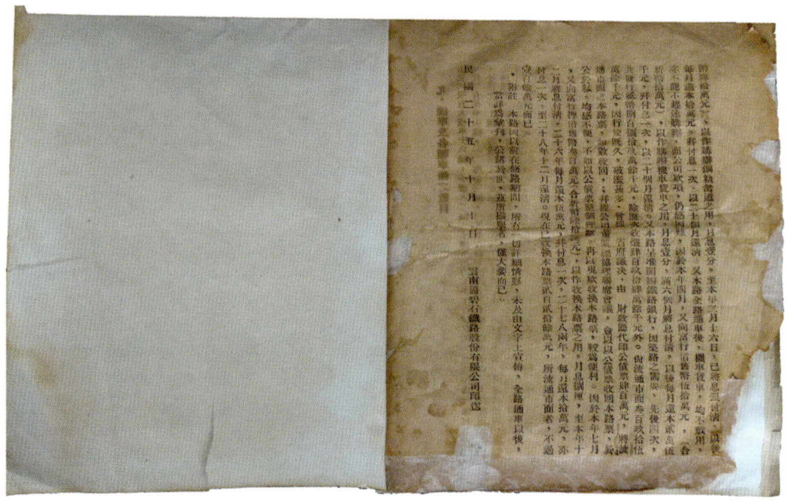

217 个碧铁路银行存款总簿

Bank Financial Savings Ledger of Gejiu-Bisezhai Railway

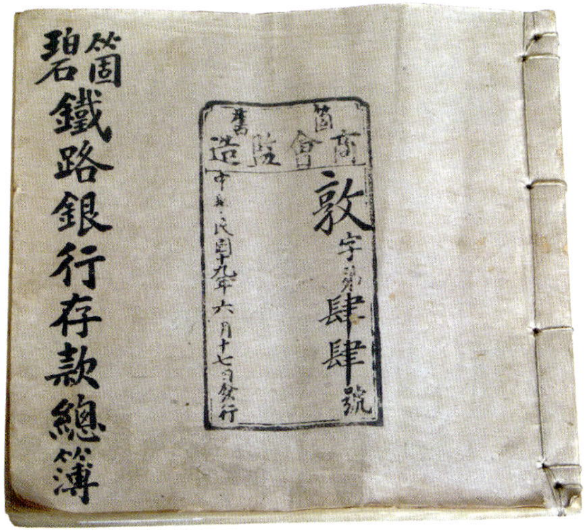

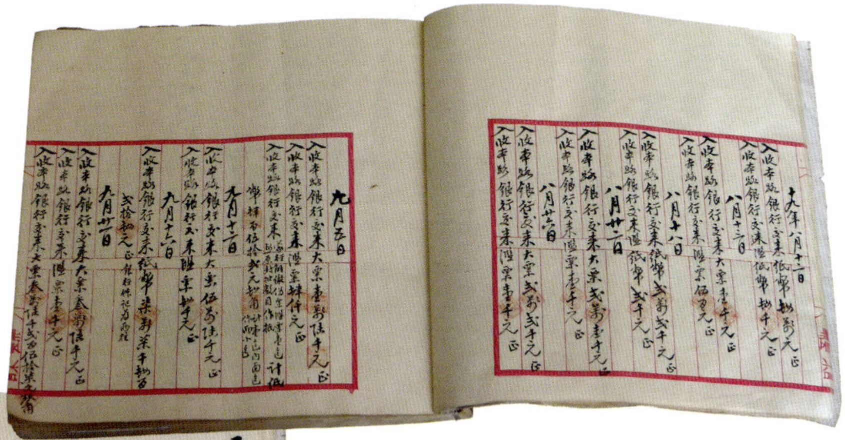

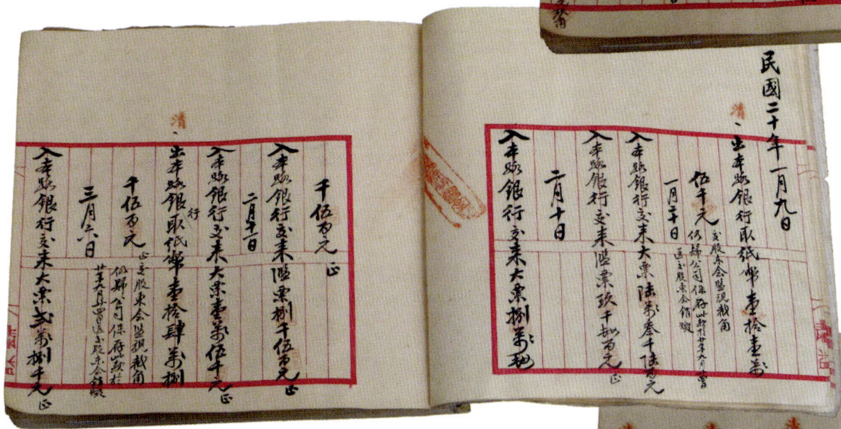

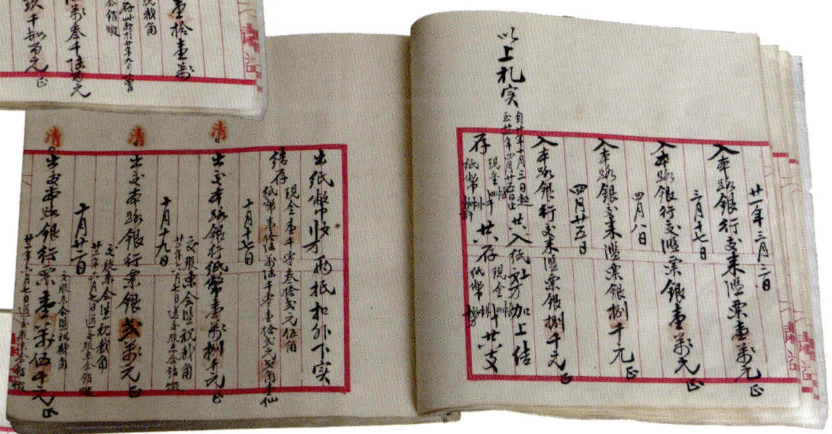

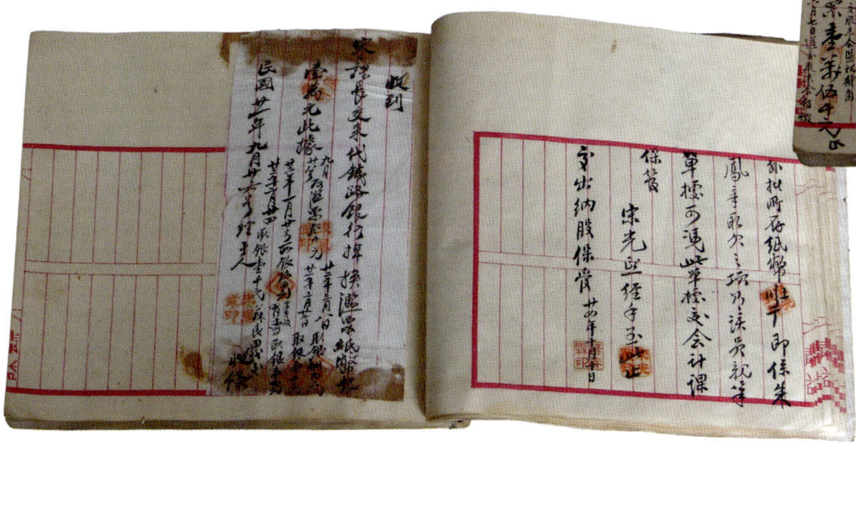

218 整理个碧铁路公司委员会报告书

The Report on Rectification of the Gejiu–Bisezhai Railway Company

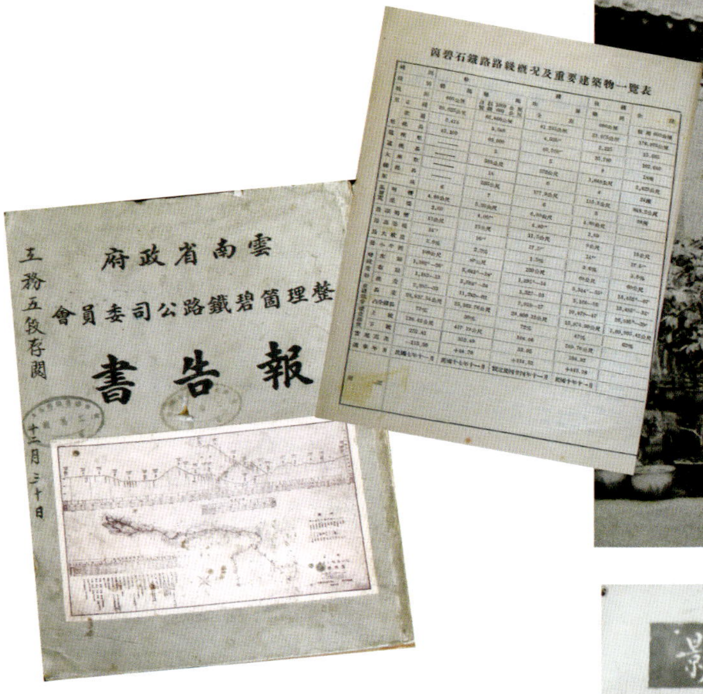

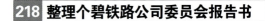

219 个碧铁路通车纪念照

Memorial Photos for the Opening of Gejiu–Bisezhai Railway

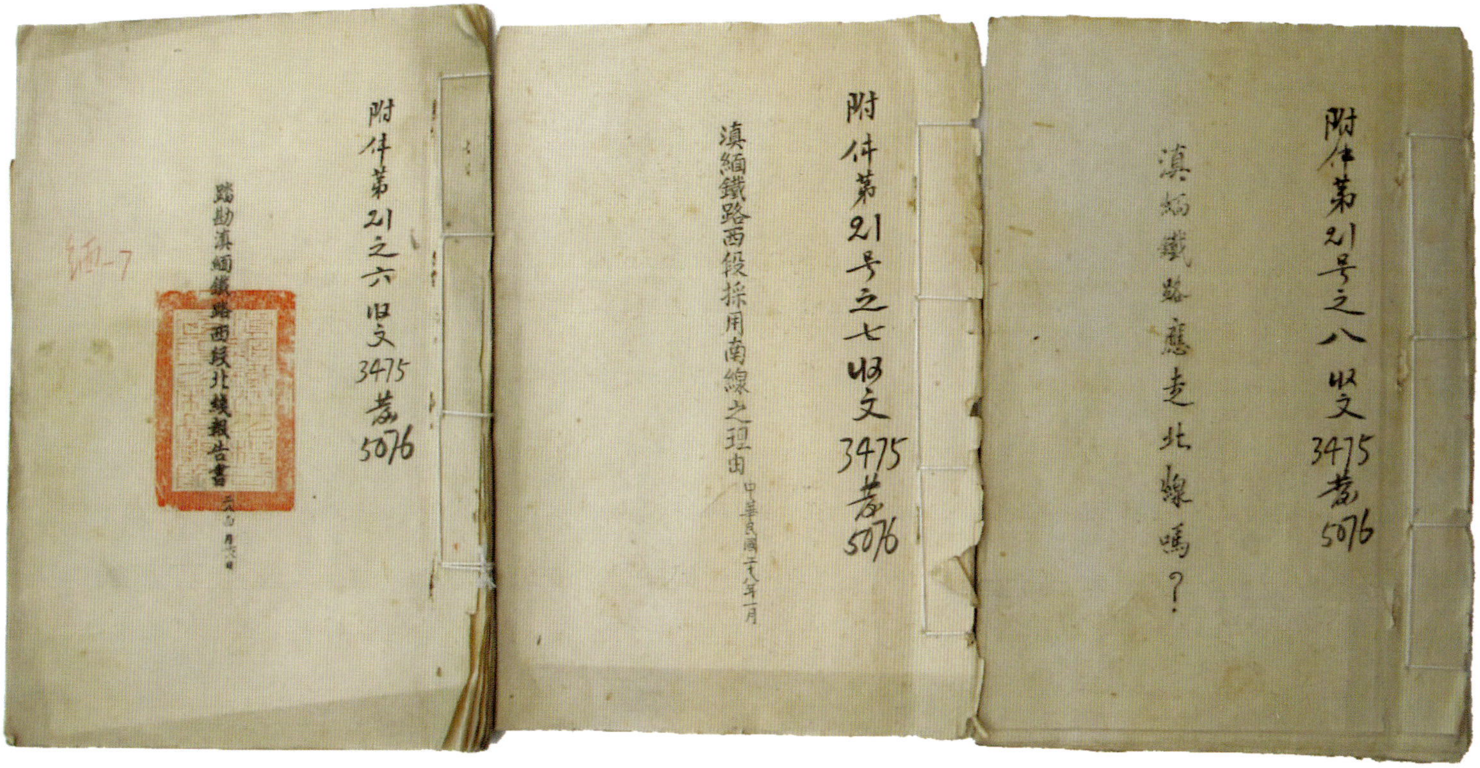

220 滇缅铁路勘测报告书（三级文物）

1. 1939年，踏勘滇缅铁路西段北线报告书。
2. 1939年，滇缅铁路西段采用南线之理由。
3. 1939年，滇缅铁路应走北线吗?

Survey Report on Yunnan–Myanmar Railway（National Grade–three Cultural Relic）

1. Survey of Northern Line of the Eastern Yunnan- Myanmar Railway (1939)
2. Reasons Why Southern Line Should Be Adopted on the Eastern Yunnan-Myanmar Railway (1939)
3. Should Yunnan–Myanmar Railway Go North Line? (1939)

CHAPPEE & FILS

第10章 Article tenth

文化遗存 Cultural Remains

一百年来，云南铁路在时间流逝中经历建与毁的轮回，在岁月蹉跎里见证盛与衰的沧桑。作为一种新型运输方式，它深刻地影响和改变了其经过的地方，也深受其经过的地方影响和熏陶着，在云南高原的红土地上培育了属于自己的独特文化。当拂去时间的尘埃，撩开历史的面纱，我们可以从中解读云南铁路生生不息的文化基因，破译它奋发图强的精神密码，诠释它蓬勃发展的内在动力。

Over the past century, experiencing the circle of construction and damages, Yunnan railway has seen ups and downs. As a new means of transportation, it cast profound impacts on the lands where it runs, and in return influenced by the cultural environment here to form its own unique characters on this red highland of Yunnan. Flicking the dust of time and unveiling the mask of history, we clear see a picture of cultural genes growing on Yunnan railway and read its codes so as to understand the impetus to vigorously develop.

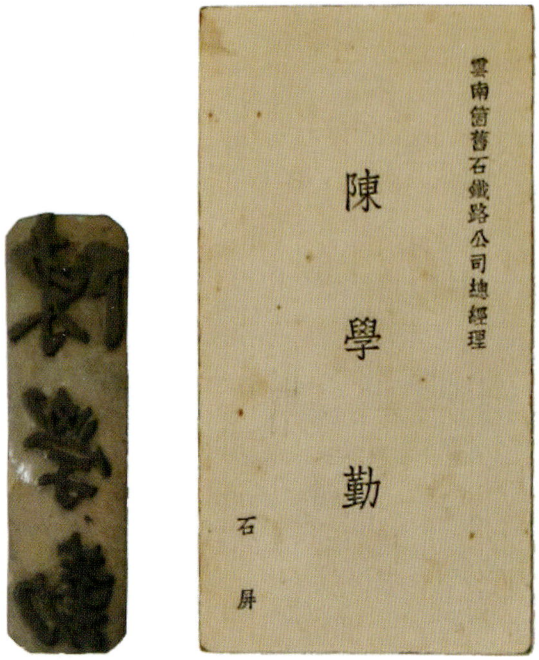

221 个碧石铁路公司末任总经理陈学勤的条章和名片

The Seal and Name Card of Chen Xueqin–the Last General Manager of Gejiu–Bisezhai–Shiping Railway Company

222 个碧石铁路1936年通车纪念章（二级文物）

The Memorial Badge of the Opening of Gejiu–Bisezhai–Shiping Railway（National Grade–two Cultural Relic）

223 个碧石铁路公司证章（三级文物）

The Badge of Gejiu–Bisezhai–Shiping Railway Company（National Grade–three Cultural Relic）

224 暖水瓶

年代：1910年　　产地：法国

Thermos Bottle

Year: 1910　　Place of production: France

225 手摇铜铃

Shaking Copper Bell

226 毛瑟枪（三级文物）

年代：19世纪　　产地：德国

Mauser Made in Europe of 19th Century
（National Grade-three Cultural Relic）

Year: 19th century

Place of production: Germany

227 脚镣手铐

Shackles and Manacles

228 活字印刷铅字

Typography Typeface

229 昂德伍德英文打字机

年代：1930年　　产地：美国

Underwood Typewriter

Year: 1930　　Place of production: U.S.A

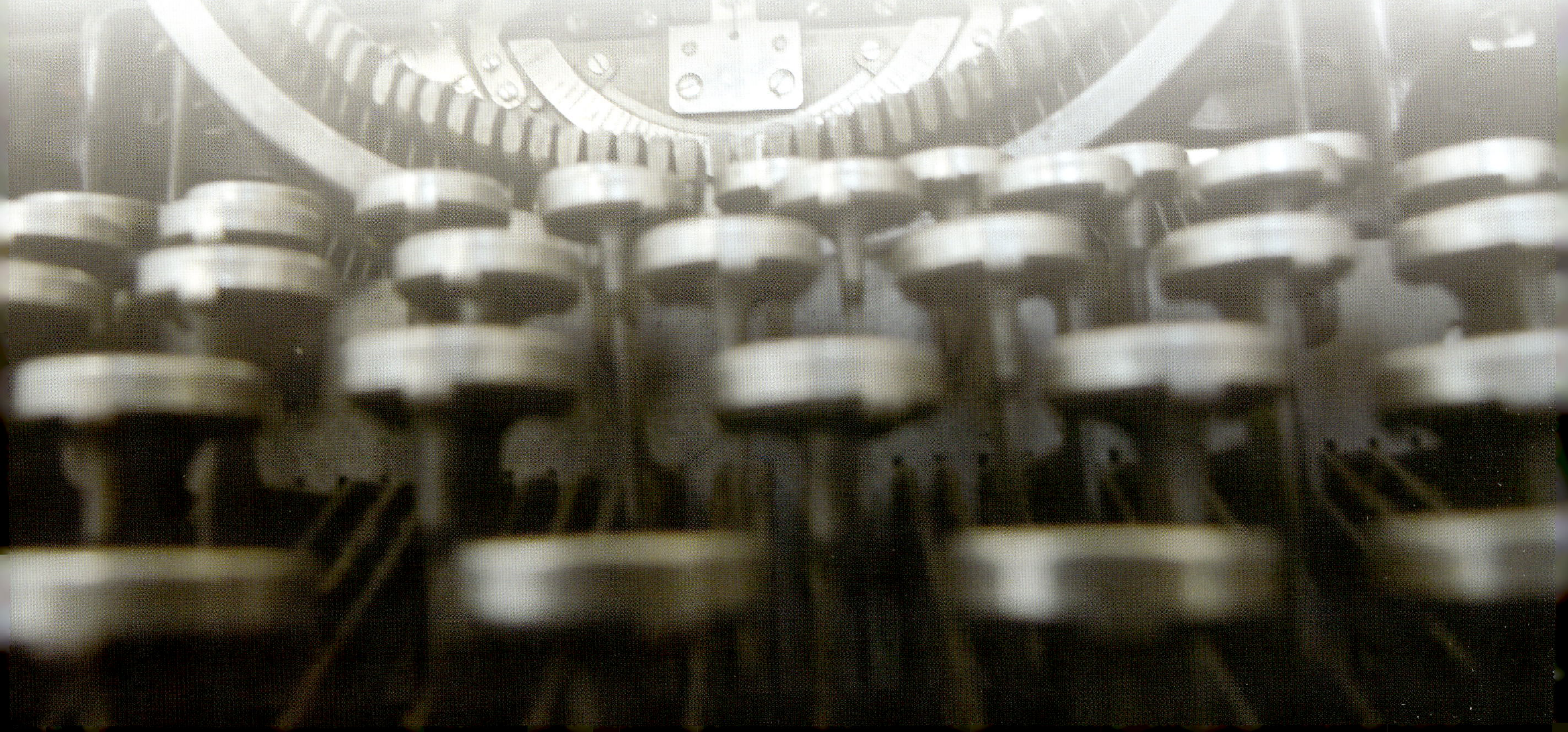

230 美国打字机

The American Typewriter

231 德国手摇机械计算器

The Hand-shaking Calculator of Germany

232 美国手摇机械计算器

The Hand-shaking Calculator of America

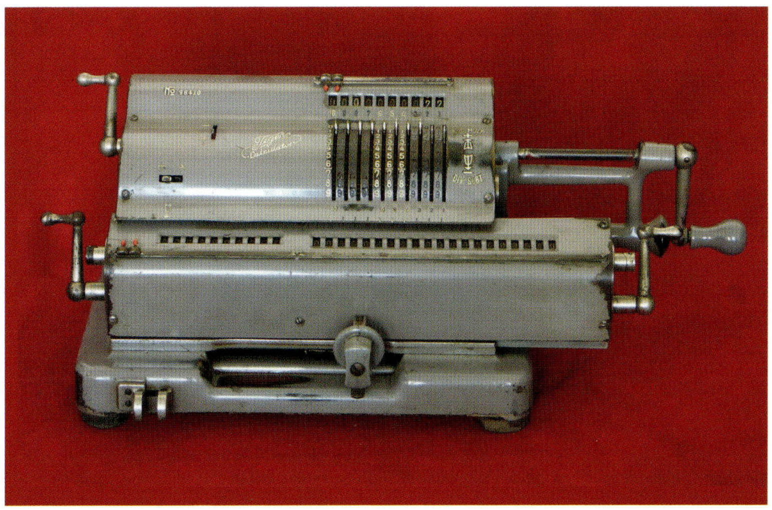

233 法式站房脊梁瓦片

年代：1910年　　产地：法国

Tiling of France Station

Year: 1910　　Place of production: France

234 法国站房瓦片

年代：1910年　　产地：法国马赛

Tiling of France Station

Year: 1910　　Place of production: Marseille, France

235 法式瓦片

Tiling of France

236 法式瓦片

Tiling of France

237 法式站房地砖

Ground Brick of French Style in Station House

238 青花瓷花瓶

年代：清朝

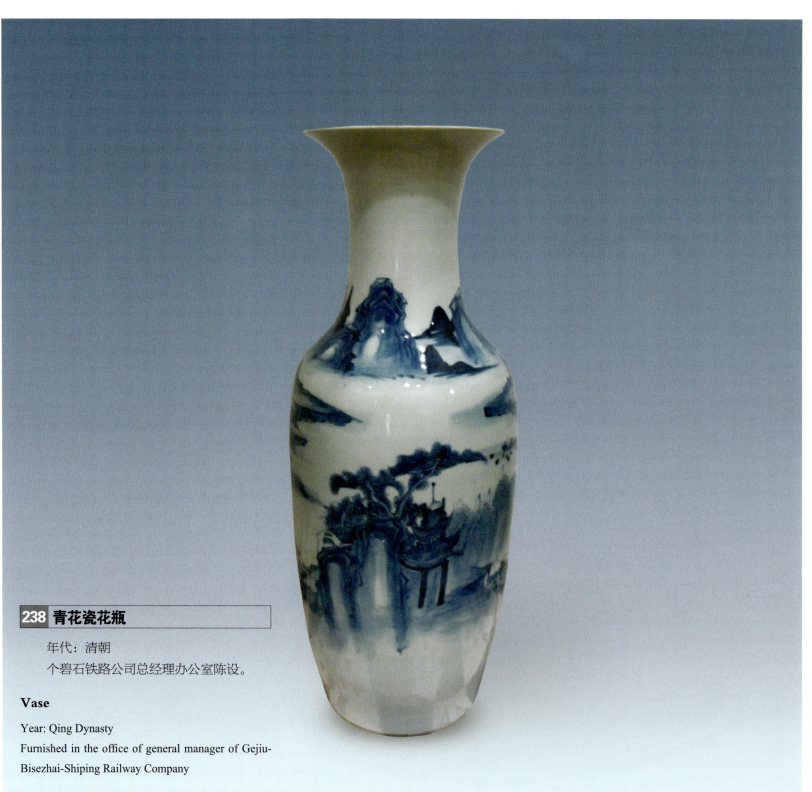

个碧石铁路公司总经理办公室陈设。

Vase

Year: Qing Dynasty

Furnished in the office of general manager of Gejiu-Bisezhai-Shiping Railway Company

239 青花瓷花盆

年代：清朝

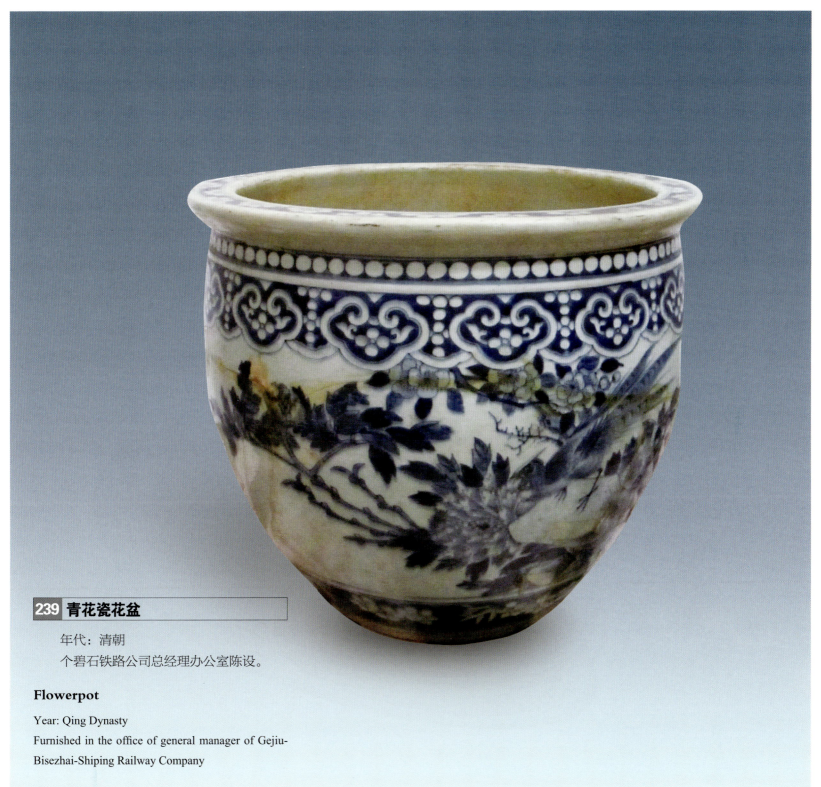

个碧石铁路公司总经理办公室陈设。

Flowerpot

Year: Qing Dynasty

Furnished in the office of general manager of Gejiu-Bisezhai-Shiping Railway Company

240 方茶几

滇越铁路法式家具。

Tea Table

French furniture of Yunnan-Vietnam Railway

241 半圆木茶几

滇越铁路法式家具。

Half Round Timber Table

French furniture of Yunnan-Vietnam Railway

242 票柜

滇越铁路法式家具。

A Ticket-selling Counter

French furniture of Yunnan-Vietnam Railway

243 办公条桌及附柜

滇越铁路法式家具。

Desk and Cabinet

French furniture of Yunnan-Vietnam Railway

244 中式嵌大理石梅花桌（三级文物）

个碧石铁路总经理办公室家具。

Chinese Style Table Inlaid with Marble Plum（National Grade-three Cultural Relic）

Furnished in the office of general manager of Gejiu-Bisezhai-Shiping Railway Company

245 中式茶几（三级文物）

滇越铁路中式家具。

Tea Tables of Chinese Style（National Grade-three Cultural Relic）

Chinese furniture of Yunnan-Vietnam Railway

246 中式椅子（三级文物）

滇越铁路中式家具。

Chairs of Chinese Style（National Grade-three Cultural Relic）

Chinese furniture of Yunnan-Vietnam Railway

247 长沙发、长条桌

1960年，中国国家主席刘少奇访问越南，乘坐米轨601公务车使用的沙发及长条桌。

The Lounge and Table

The lounge and table were used by Liu Shaoqi, then Chairman of China, when he visited Vietnam on No.601 meter-gauge official train in 1960.

248 长条椅子（三级文物）

1915年，个碧石铁路公司会议室使用的长条椅子。

Long Wooden Chair (National Grade-three Cultural Relic)

Long wooden chairs used in the meeting room of Gejiu-Bisezhai-Shiping Railway Company.

249 角柜

滇越铁路使用的法式家具。

年代：1910年　　产地：越南

The Corner Table

French furniture of Yunnan-Vietnam Railway

Year: 1910　　Place of production: Vietnam

250 法式高立柜

滇越铁路使用的法式家具。

年代：1910年　　产地：法国

The Tall Closet of French Style

French furniture of Yunnan-Vietnam Railway

Year: 1910　　Place of production: France

251 重铊式三面钟（二级文物）

这是1910年法国制造的重铊式三面钟，设于滇越铁路主要车站。室外的两面钟为子钟，面向月台两侧，为旅客指示时间；室内的一面为母钟，供车站工作人员使用。

Three-sided Clock（National Grade-two Cultural Relic）

This perpendicular clock that was made in France in 1910 was fixed on the building of main station of Yunnan-Vietnam Railway. Two sides of the clock faced the platform to show passengers time while the main side faced the staff office was for staffs to use.

（正面）
Front

（背面）
Back

（正面）
Front

（背面）
Back

252 洋行用铜钟

滇越铁路外国洋行使用。

The Clock Used in the Foreign Firm

Used in Foreign Firms of Yunnan Vietnam Railway

253 挂钟

年代：1920年　　产地：中国

A Wall Clock

Year: 1920　　Place of production: China

254 法式带镜双门柜（三级文物）

年代：1920年　　产地：法国

French Style Cabinet with Two Doors and Mirror（National Grade-three Cultural Relic）

Year: 1920　　Place of production: France

255 保险柜

年代：1920年　　产地：法国

The Safe

Year: 1920　　Place of production: France

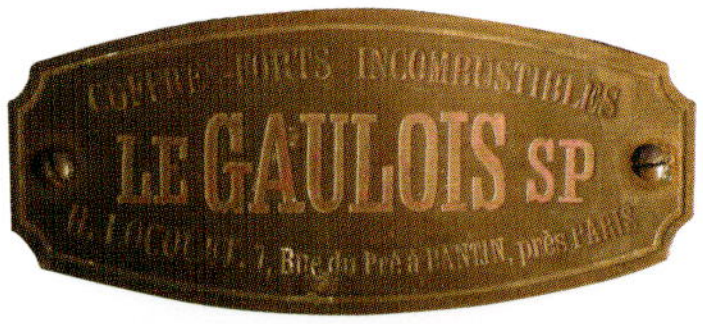

256 保险柜

年代：1910年　　产地：法国

The Safe

Year: 1910　　Place of production: France

257 磅秤砣

产地：法国

The Scale of Thallium

Place of production: France

258 水龙头盒

产地：法国

Water Tap Box

Place of production: France

259 磅秤

年代：1910　　产地：法国

Ground Balance

Year: 1910　　Place of production: France

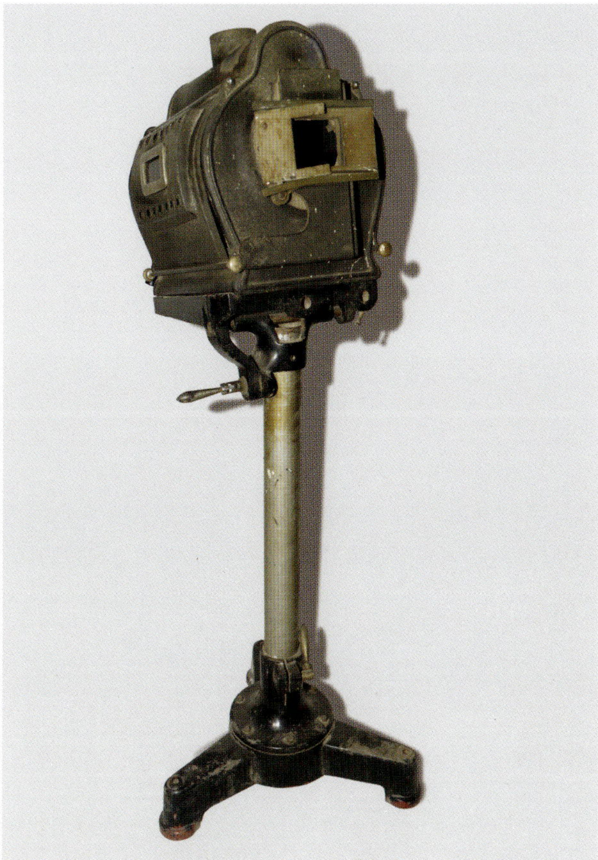

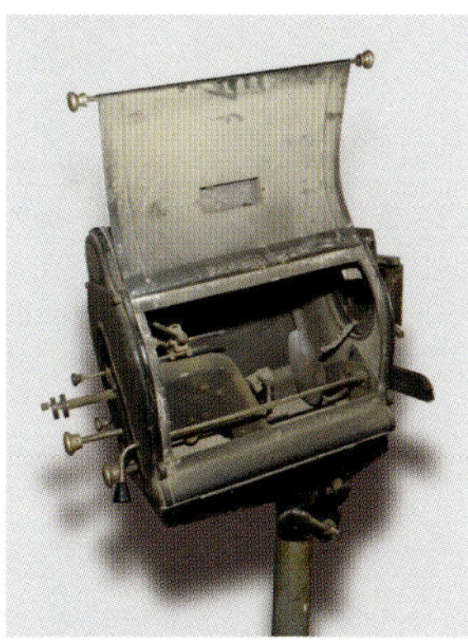

260 幻灯片放映机

年代：1950年　　产地：中国上海

Slide Projector

Year: 1950　　Place of production: Shanghai, China

261 电影放映机

年代：1950年　　产地：中国哈尔滨

Cinematograph

Year: 1950　　Place of production: Haerbin, China

Time flies. A hundred years has slipped away.

Weighing the gains and losses, we feel pleased although some pity cannot be ignored.

On one hand, we are grateful that Yunnan railway has not lost its unique genes in the fast development, as a ship wisely keep its direction to avoid deviation. No matter how to expand and upgrade, Yunnan railway has always been marked by its own history and culture.

On the other hand, we are surprised that according to the principle of harmonizing operation with protection, a lot of ancient architectures and old equipments by the railway have been carefully protected.

Some of them are exhibited in the museum as valuable treasures, and some are named important units of cultural relics protection, faithfully guarding their hometown. It is the relics, like "Inverted-V Bridge" with ingenious design (Note: This bridge is popularly called Le Viaduc de Faux-Namti in French), Jijie station combining the element of the eastern and western, the colorful railway stations in Bisezhai village and numerous small stations with red tiles and yellow walls in the sunset, that backup our enduring history and keep our times warm.

第11章 文物保护单位

Article eleventh

Units of Cultural Relics Protection

时光荏苒，岁月如梭，100年匆匆而过。

盘点我们的收获，打捞曾经的失去，我们难免有丝丝遗憾，但更多的是欣慰！

我们庆幸：在时间的长河里前行没有偏离航道失去自我，在快速发展中没有丢掉自己的基因。云南铁路无论怎样扩展经纬和提升标高，始终对自己的历史有一份储存。

我们惊喜：由于遵循了“在运营中保护和在保护中运营”的原则，铁路沿线的众多老建筑老设备受到很好的呵护，其中的经典，有的成为珍贵文物陈列在博物馆，有的则成为了国家和省市区县的“重点文物保护单位”，忠贞地守望着她的故地。匠心独运的人字桥、中西合璧的鸡街站、璀璨多姿的碧色寨站区建筑群落，还有夕阳余辉映照下许许多多铁路沿线红瓦黄墙的小站，备份着我们历久弥新的历史，温暖着我们浓烈醇香的岁月情怀……

01 全国重点文物保护单位
Units of National Key Cultural Relics Protection

262 屏边五家寨铁路钢梁桥（“人字桥”）

屏边五家寨铁路钢梁桥建在滇越铁路波渡箐车站与倮姑车站之间，位于云南省屏边县五家寨，是横跨四岔河深谷的钢拱桥，距谷底有100余米，两岸为陡峭的绝壁，桥长67.15米，桥重179.5吨，由法国工程师保尔·波登（Paul Bodin）设计，由法国巴底纽勒（Batignoller）建筑公司建造，于1907年3月10日开工，1908年12月6日竣工。

该桥为双重式结构，下部为三铰人字拱，拱臂底部支承于山腰间的铸钢球形支座上，顶部合拢后联接于钢枢上，形似一个张开臂膀、巍然屹立的钢铁巨人，所以被人们俗称为“人字桥”。

“人字桥”运营百年，至今仍完好如初，风姿依旧。2006年，因独具匠心的设计、雄伟壮观的身姿、坚实可靠的质量和弥足珍贵的文物价值，被确定为全国“重点文物保护单位”。

人字桥
The Inverted V-shape Bridge

今天的人字桥全景
The Full View of the Inverted ∧-shape Bridge Today

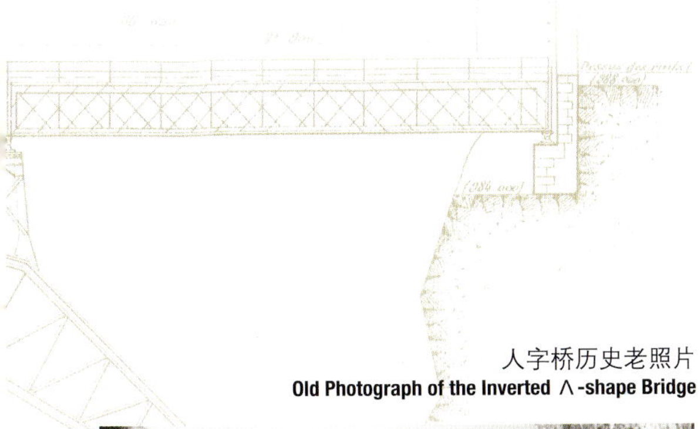

人字桥历史老照片
Old Photograph of the Inverted Λ-shape Bridge

The Pingbian Wujiazhai Rail Steel Girder Bridge (“The Inverted Λ-shape Bridge”)

The Pingbian Wujiazhai Rail Steel Girder Bridge is located at Wujiazhai village in Pingbian town of Yunnan province, between Boduqing Station and Luogu Station on Yunnan–Vietnam Railway. It is a steel arch bridge across the deep valley of the Sicha River, more than 100 meters high above the valley bottom. On both shores of it stand extremely steep cliffs. This bridge is 67.15 meters long and weighs 179.5 tons. It was designed by a French engineer called Paul Bodin, and built by Batignoller, a French construction company. The project started on March 10th, 1907, and was completed on December 6th, 1908.

列车通过人字桥
Trains Passing the Inverted Λ-shape Bridge

This bridge is double-structured, the lower part of which is a three-hinged arch, inverted Λ-shape like, and propping on the cast steel global bottoms built on the mountainsides while closing to connect with the upper steel bridge. It looks like a steel giant who stands majestically with arms open. This is why it is also called “Ren–like Bridge”. (“Ren”, a Chinese character, means a person. The configuration of it “人” is similar to an inverted “V” in English.)

The Inverted Λ-shape Bridge has been in operation for more than a century, still keeping itself in a good state like a new one. It was put on the list of “National key cultural relics protection units” in 2006, because of its inventive design, grand body, reliable quality and precious cultural value.

263 鸡街车站

鸡街车站位于云南省个旧市鸡街镇境内，为原个碧石寸轨铁路的车站，1970年，个碧石寸轨铁路大部分改造为与滇越铁路相连的米轨铁路后，其中心里程为蒙(自)宝(秀)铁路27.73千米处。但鸡街车站仍保留寸轨铁路运营至1990年12月31日止，现已退出历史舞台，成为米轨铁路人永远的记忆……

2006 年，鸡街车站被确定为国家“重点文物保护单位”。

The Jijie Railway Station

The Jijie Railway Station is located at Jijie Town, Gejiu City in Yunnan Province. It was a station on Gejiu-Bisezhai-Shiping 600mm-gauge Railway. In 1970, when the most parts of Gejiu-Bisezhai-Shiping 600mm-gauge Railway was transformed to 1000mm rail linked with Yunnan–Vietnam Railway, the station was located at the point of 27.73 kilometers on Mengzi–Baoxiu Railway. However, the Jijie Railway Station did not quit its operation of 600mm-gauge railway until the end of 1990. Today, it has stepped down from the stage of history and stayed in the memory of 600mm-gauge railway people forever……

In 2006, the Jijie Railway Station was included in the list of “Units of National key cultural relics protection”.

今天的鸡街车站
The Jijie Railway Station today

鸡街车站旧照片
An old photograph of the Jijie Railway station

264 碧色寨车站

碧色寨车站位于云南省蒙自市草坝镇碧色寨村。车站以法式建筑为主，辅以中西合璧的建筑，并伴有当地民居，样式多样，风格异彩纷呈。

碧色寨车站是滇越铁路米轨与个碧石铁路寸轨进行货物换装和旅客换乘的车站，对研究我国铁路发展史有着重要价值。1987年被列为云南省重点文物保护单位，2013年，被列入国家“重点文物保护单位”。

The Bisezhai Railway Station

The Bisezhai Railway Station is located at Bise Village, Caoba Town, Mengzi City in Yunnan province. With a main style of French architectures, the station also includes some buildings combining eastern and western styles, and even some local residences, which makes the station diverse in styles and thus beautiful.

碧色寨车站旧照片

Old photograph of the Bisezhai Railway station

The Bisezhai Railway Station was a station for cargos and passengers to transfer between Yunnan–Vietnam Railway and Gejiu-Bisezhai-Shiping Railway. As a result, it plays an essential role in the research in the development history of Chinese railways. The Bisezhai Railway Station was titled “the unit of Yunnan provincial key cultural relics protection” in 1987, and “the unit of national key cultural relics protection” in 2013.

02 云南省重点文物保护单位
Units of Yunnan Provincial Key Cultural Relics Protection

265 芷村车站

芷村站，旧称迷拉地车站，建于1909年，位于云南省蒙自市芷村镇境内，铁路中心里程位于滇越铁路312.46千米处。整个车站至今仍完整保留6幢法式建筑，2012年被列为云南省重点文物保护单位。

The Zhicun Railway Station

Located at Zhicun Village of Mengzi City, Yunnan Province, the Zhicun Railway Station, formerly called the Miladi Railway Station, was built in 1909. The station is at the point of 312.46 kilometers on Yunnan–Vietnam Railway. Up to now, six French architectures have remained there in an intact state. In 2012, the station was included in the list of "Units of Yunnan Provincial key cultural relics protection".

芷村车站
The Zhicun Railway Station

历史上的白寨大桥
An old photograph of the Baizhai Bridge

266 白寨大桥

该桥位于滇越铁路湾塘站与白寨站区间，铁路中心里程位于381.62千米处。始建于1907年9月15日，1908年3月10日建成。桥体为上承箱式钢铁高架桥，桥墩为8个钢塔架，其中：1号墩高10.30米，2号墩高26米，3、5、6、7号墩均高34米，4号墩高33米，8号墩高32米。桥梁为曲线布局，桥长136米，总重374吨。1940年因战火拆毁。1958年修复，桥墩改为石砌结构。2012年被列为云南省重点文物保护单位。

The Baizhai Bridge

This bridge is located at the point of 381.62 kilometers on Yunnan–Vietnam Railway, between the Wantang Station and the Baizhai Station. It started constructing on September 15th, 1907, and was completed on March 10th, 1908. The bridge is a steel viaduct of deck-box structure, the piers of which are eight steel towers, including No.1 pier of a height of 10.30 meters, No.2 pier of a height of 26 meters, No.3, 5, 6, and 7 piers of a same height of 34 meters, No.4 pier of a height of 33 meters, and No.8 pier of a height of 32 meters. The bridge stretches in a curve, with a length of 136 meters and a weight of 374 tons. In 1940, it was unfortunately damaged in wars. When rebuilt in 1958, the piers were remade of stones. The bridge was put on the list of "Units of Yunnan Provincial key cultural relics protection" in 2012.

现在的白寨大桥
The Baizhai Bridge today

03 州、市以及县（市）文物保护单位

Units of State, City and County (City) Cultural Relics Protection

267 玉林山七孔桥

玉林山七孔桥位于滇越铁路249.72千米处，因所处位置靠近开远市玉林山村，且有七孔桥墩而得名。该桥建于1908年，由法国巴底纽勒（Batignoller）公司设计建造，桥长95.8米，宽4.4米，桥墩最高21米，最低14米，坡度21‰，为七孔高架石桥。

经百年风雨冲刷，桥墩逐渐出现松动。从20世纪60年代起，铁路工程部门先后对七孔桥进行拱顶钢夹板加固、桥拱水泥加固等数次维修，增强了桥体的稳固性。

玉林山七孔桥，1983年被列为开远市文物保护单位。

开远玉林山七孔石拱桥
The Yulinshan Seven-arch Bridge

The Yulinshan Seven-arch Bridge

The Yulinshan Seven-arch Bridge is located at the point of 249.72 kilometers on Yunnan–Vietnam Railway. Nearby Yulinshan Village and with seven arches, it is named the Yulinshan Seven-arch Bridge. This bridge was built in 1908 by Batignoller, a French company. It is a seven-arch stone viaduct, 95.8 meters long, 4.4 meters wide. The length of its piers ranges from 14 meters to 21 meters, with a 21‰ slope.

Through winds and storms for more than a century, the piers were gradually loosening. Since 1960s, in order to strengthen the stability of the bridge, the railway engineering administration has made several maintenances like reinforcement of arches with steel plywood and cement.

The Yulinshan Seven-arch Bridge was named “the Unit of Kaiyuan City Cultural Relics Protection”.

268 小龙潭大桥

1909年建成，桥梁专业名称为穿式桁架钢梁桥。桥体主跨为51.5米的桁架钢梁结构，主跨两端分别与1~3孔跨度为10米的石拱桥相连，桥梁全长100余米，桥梁总重量为109吨。因桥体结构美观，被当地的人们爱称为“花桥”，现为开远市文物保护单位。

Xiaolongtan Bridge

This Bridge was built in 1909, called "through steel truss bridge" in architectural terms. The main body of the bridge is a steel truss structure 51.5 meters long, both ends of which connect to a stone arch bridge that is 10 meters long and with 1~3 holes. The bridge is more than 100 meters long and weighs 109 tons. Due to its artistic look, it is called "Hua Bridge" by local people. (The Chinese character "Hua" means a beautiful flower.) Xiaolongtan Bridge is a Unit of Kaiyuan City Cultural Relics Protection.

小龙潭大桥旧照
An old photograph of Xiaolongtan Bridge

现在的小龙潭大桥
Xiaolongtan Bridge today

编后语

编辑完成这本文物图册，仿佛拜读了一部经典，让我们油然产生了对历史的敬畏。书中的每一个静态文物好似注入了鲜活的生命内涵，导引着我们步入蜿蜒于喀斯特地貌和红土高原之上的云南铁路，回眸它走过的每一个历史驿站，从百年轨迹中认识云南铁路的今昔，领略一代代铁路人的奋斗风采，获得对未来发展的心灵启迪和精神振奋。

这些蕴含铁路物质文明和精神文化魅力的文物，形象生动地成为了与中国铁路及云南边疆共生发展的历史符号和极富思辨哲理的文化语汇，多个角度地展现了云南铁路折射的文明之光对历史时空的穿透，异彩纷呈地解读了红土高原多元民族神韵在铁路文化价值中的承载。

追怀既往，奋扬开来。我们站在当下，向着百年云南铁路的源头回眸而望，许多人和事早已悄然无息地消融在时间的长河里，有的沉淀在某个时间的节点已无法打捞，有的经历时间的冲刷仍然坚守着原来的坐标。小溪小河的支流也许改道或淹没了，而大江东去的主流则一直往前，因为云南铁路的发展如同正矢量的时间注定永远大踏步地前进！

历经百年沧桑巨变的云南铁路，而今已阔步成长为迈向世界的钢铁大道，成为中国面向东南亚和南亚开放桥头堡的重要支撑。站在百年历史的沃土之上，云南铁路正奋力追赶奔流向前的美好明天！

由于本图册涉及的文物内容较广，时间跨度较长，资料搜集不全，谬误和不当之处，敬请各位专家和读者指正。

最后，由衷地感谢为收集保存文物和创建云南铁路博物馆作出贡献的所有单位和个人！真诚地向为编辑出版本文物图册提供支持和帮助的所有单位和个人致敬！

编者

2014年3月 春

Postscript

Having this album finished is just like reading a classic, inspiring us to be in owe of history. Vivacious lives infused into each seemingly silent cultural relics lead us through Yunnan railway that winds its way on Karst landforms and red highlands. Looking back every stop it walks, we understand the past and present of Yunnan railway, appreciate the spirit of generations of railway workers and furthermore gain the enlightenment and confidence of the future.

These cultural relics containing both material and spiritual civilization serve as vivid historic marks and cultural languages that tell development of Chinese railway in borderlands. They show the light of civilization of Yunnan railway penetrating the history clouds in different aspects, and demonstrate the multi-ethnic culture of this red highland transmitted in a brilliant manner.

Standing by the river of the past, we get brave to set out for the future. When we give a glance back of the source of Yunnan railway, countless people and events have already vanished in the sea of time. Some perhaps cannot be found any longer, while some still stick to their coordinates. Some branches might change but what is unchanged is the mainstream since Yunnan railway will inevitably stride forward as time makes rapid headway that never backs!

Through impressive changes in the past century, Yunnan railway, a steel avenue leading to the world, has grown an essential support of the opening bridgehead where China faces Southeast Asia and South Asia. Planted in the fertile soil of a history more than one hundred years, Yunnan railway is striving to a better tomorrow!

Since large amounts of cultural relics and a very long time span are involved in this album, it is unavoidable to leave out some information and make mistakes. Any improvement suggestion is welcomed.

At last, sincerely thanks for units and individuals who collected the cultural relics and built Yunnan Railway Museum! Sincerely thanks for the support and help of compiling this album!

Editors

Spring, March, 2014